Discipleship

IN
GOD'S ETERNAL PURPOSE

by Jerry Jones

A Biblical Study of the
Design, Demand, and Demonstration
of Being a Disciple of Jesus Christ

This book is dedicated to my wife, Claudette, and to my three children: Angela, Kris Anne, and Charles Allen. Without their encouragement, sacrifice and confidence in me, this book and my ministry for Jesus would not be possible. Home has always been my "oasis" from the pressures of preaching, teaching and traveling. I am especially grateful to a loving heavenly Father who has been patient with His son as he has attempted to grow into His image.

A special thanks to Peggie Baker for her typing skills, her belief in the potential of this book, her good suggestions and her quiet, gentle spirit.

Commendation is in order to Wally Hodge of Memphis, Tennessee, for his cover design.

This book is written with the prayer that God will use it to help others as much as the material has helped me. I trust it will assist in achieving the goal of ministry (Colossians 1:28).

All scripture references are taken from the New American Standard Bible (NAS) unless otherwise noted. Other versions used are NIV (New International Version) and RSV (Revised Standard Version).

Many ideas and illustrations in this book have been gleaned from listening to lectures, tapes, reading books and articles and from conversations with fellow disciples. Proper footnoting of the original source of every idea was an impossible task. Some of the original sources were either never known or forgotten. I felt that excessive footnotes would detract from the readability of the book. The "originality" of the book is found in the arrangement and thrust. However, a special thanks is given to Dr. Carroll Osborn and Jim Woodroof for their help in understanding the life and teachings of Jesus.

Additional books can be ordered by writing Jerry Jones, 1 Harding Drive, Searcy, Arkansas 72143.

Table of Contents

Discipleship in God's Eternal Purpose
Introduction

One of the most difficult questions facing man in the 20th century is, "What does it mean to follow Jesus?" Are you really following Jesus or merely going through some Christian pantomime? Have two thousand years of religious movements, men and writings so confused the meaning of discipleship that no one is really following the man from Nazareth? These questions and others similar to them led to the writing of this book.

Every sincere disciple seeks some confirmation that he is what God purposed him to be. Comparing ourselves with those around us who profess faith in Jesus is not enough to confirm that everything "is well with our souls." Merely feeling good about ourselves leaves something to be desired in our quest to know if we *really* belong to Him.

The quest to know if I am His has to be answered in the revelation of the will of God to man in the scriptures. My search to know led me first to the book of Mark and then branched out to the rest of the Bible. A diligent study of the word and a daily prayer for wisdom which comes from above led me to the most exciting discovery (what it means to be His) in my ministry for Him. I could not believe it had taken me so many years to see what now appears to be so clear. Discipleship will never have the same meaning for me because I have a direction and confirmation which I have never had.

As a background for my search for the meaning of discipleship, Ephesians' concept of the eternal purpose of God served as the foundation.

The Bible affirms that God does not act on the spur of the moment but has purposed the future from the very beginning.

> Just as He chose us in Him before the foundation of the world, that we should be holy and blameless before Him (Ephesians 1:4).

The theme of Ephesians is Christ, the head of the church. The first three chapters show the church in the eternal purpose. God is set forth as the architect of the great purpose. God's determination and purpose were formed before the foundation of the world (Ephesians 1:4). In this purpose God chose us and predestined us (Ephesians 1:4-5), and we became the elect of God (Romans 8:33). As individuals we can choose to be of the chosen, and elect to be of the elect. The purpose of God's plan for man was basically two-fold: (1) Man might be saved (holy, blameless and sons); (2) God might be glorified (Ephesians 1:6, 12, and 14).

In order for God's purpose to work, Jesus had to be involved. Jesus became the consummation of all things that it took to save the world.

> With a view to an administration suitable to the fulness of the times, that is, the summing up of all things in Christ, things in the heavens and things upon the earth. (Ephesians 1:10)

What man has in Christ is manifold: (1) spiritual blessings (1:3); (2) God's chosen (1:4); (3) sonship (1:5); (4) grace (1:6); (5) redemption (1:7); (6) inheritance (1:10-11); (7) sealed with the Holy Spirit (1:13-14).

The word "purpose" is used as a verb (1:9) and as a noun (1:11). When Paul said that the manifold wisdom of God is made known through the church (3:10), he connected it with the eternal purpose.

> In order that the manifold wisdom of God might now be made known through the *church* to the rulers and the authorities in the heavenly places. This was in accordance with the *eternal purpose* which He carried out in Christ Jesus our Lord (Ephesians 3:10-11).

Our place in the purpose was determined by God before the creation.

> For we are His workmanship, created in Christ Jesus for good works, which God prepared beforehand (in advance, NIV), that we should walk in them (Ephesians 2:10).

God desires His workmanship (which has been created for good works), to do good works. We are not saved *by* works, but *for* works. It is thrilling to be a part of something that is older than the world!

Since the church is a demonstration of the wisdom of God and the eternal purpose of God, it stands to reason that the followers and members of the eternal purpose of God (the church) are also a part of the plan of God. The history of the Bible shows that God has not left man to his own imaginations, but He has set forth a plan for him. If we are to actively participate in the eternal purpose, we must seek to find out how God wants us to live for Him.

To even hint that God did not have a plan from the beginning for those who would follow Him is to make a mockery of the greatness of God. The command of Jesus to follow Him had its roots when God formed the world from nothing. Man has never been left to his own thinking, but God has always been directing him in the pathway that was best for him. Man is the only creation made in the image of God. The uniqueness of man in the realm of creation is further borne out in the purpose God has for him in his following.

You will never feel good about your life until you are functioning in the sphere for which you were created. Birds were created to live in the air, fish in water and man in a close fellowship with his creator. You will never know this sphere of fellowship until you understand what being His disciple really entails.

Section I

Design of Discipleship

When you hear the word "disciple," what comes to mind? The word "follower" comes to my mind. However, the word carries a meaning that is greater than "follower." In ancient Greece, a disciple (*mathetes*) was considered an apprentice. When someone was learning to play the flute, he was called a disciple. A person who was training to be a doctor under a physician was called a disciple. Therefore, a disciple is more than merely a follower. He is also serving an apprenticeship under one who is more experienced than he is.

In order for one to be a disciple, he must have a teacher. This becomes clearer to us as we study the ancient Greek philosophers. The disciples were considered to be part of certain Greek schools. These were not schools as we understand schools to be today. They were schools without walls. The philosophers would gather disciples around them, and as they traveled, he would teach them. The Greeks had a word to describe these schools—*peripetetic*. This was the Greek word for "walking around."

The concept of discipleship is also found in ancient Hebrew thought. In Genesis 5:22 Enoch is described as a man who walked with God. This phraseology projects the idea that Enoch was a follower of God. Later Old Testament history shows that the prophets had their own followers. These followers were known as the "sons of the prophets" (1 Kings 20:35). These were not the biological sons of the prophets, but ones who were closely associated with the prophets. This helps to understand Paul's explanation of his educational background.

> I am a Jew, born in Tarsus of Cilicia, but brought up in the city, educated under Gamaliel, strictly according to the law of our fathers, being zealous for God, just as you all are today (Acts 22:3).

1

It was not unusual for one to identify himself by referring to the rabbi who was his teacher.

When the New Testament opens and people are identified as disciples of John or of Jesus, the terminology is not new. When Jesus' teaching attracted disciples, this was a natural response in the first century. In fact the teaching of Jesus either created disciples or enemies for the most part. The teaching of Jesus was not treated with indifference, but with acceptance or rejection. We are faced with the same decision as we see the teachings of Jesus. In our modern world, it is the fashionable thing to try to be the friend of all and the enemy of none. If Jesus made anything clear to us, it is the fact that we must decide whose disciples we are. If you fail to choose, you will find yourself in bondage to another master and not even realize it. A good example of this is the exchange Jesus had in John 8:31-34.

> Jesus therefore was saying to those Jews who had believed Him, 'If you abide in My word, then you are truly disciples of Mine; and you shall know the truth, and the truth shall make you free.' They answered Him, 'We are Abraham's offspring, and have never yet been enslaved to anyone; how is it that You say, "You shall become free?"' Jesus answered them, 'Truly, truly, I say to you, everyone who commits sin is the slave of sin.'

Jesus was offering freedom to ones who thought they were free and did not need it. They were enslaved as followers without their realizing what was taking place. Discipleship in Jesus offers you a freedom and a life that cannot be possessed in any other following. It is true that the decision is yours, but this life is the only classroom you have in which to make that decision. After you graduate, you cannot go back again. The course is over.

Chapter 1

Rooted in God

It is impossible for us to know how to be disciples without understanding our Maker. If you were asked to define man, one definition could be that man is the image of God. However what good is that definition if we do not know God. Have you ever said of someone that he is the image of his father? If you don't know his father, you don't know any more about the son than you did before. Consequently, defining what we are to be as disciples must begin by understanding the one whose image we are.

1. I Am

God is not questioned in scripture. One who says there is no God is a fool (Psalms 14:1; 53:1). When Moses was unsure as to whether or not he should go to Egypt and lead God's people out, he inquired, "Who shall I say sent me?" The answer was simply, "I am who I am" (Exodus 3:14).

The basis for ethics is rooted in the nature of God. The idea that we are to be like God is reflected in the Old and New Testaments:

> For I am the Lord your God. Consecrate yourselves therefore, and *be holy; for I am holy.* And you shall not make yourselves unclean with any of the swarming things that swarm on the earth (Leviticus 11:44).

> But like the *Holy One* who called you, *be holy* yourselves also in all your behavior (1 Peter 1:15).

In Ephesians Paul stressed God's eternal purpose—we are His workmanship, and we are to be imitators of God.

> Therefore be *imitators of God*, as beloved children (Ephesians 5:1).

A knowledge of God is basic to developing a relationship with God. When the Old Testament used "knowledge," it meant more than just "knowing about something." True knowledge carries with it a deeper understanding which is shown in an intimate relationship. When the Old Testament declared that "my people are destroyed for a lack of knowledge" (Hosea 4:6), it did not mean intellectual knowledge but relationship. When one does not know God, he will not live like God wants him to live.

> Listen, O heavens, and hear, O earth; for the Lord speaks, 'Sons I have reared and brought up, But they have revolted against Me. An ox knows its owner, And a donkey its master's manger. But *Israel does not know*, My people do not understand' (Isaiah 1:2-3).

> And just as they did not see fit to *acknowledge God* any longer, God gave them over to a depraved mind, to do those things which are not proper (Romans 1:28).

3

Not in lustful passion, like the Gentiles *who do not know God* (1 Thessalonians 4:5).

"A person comes to be like what he loves, and grows to be like what he worships."[1] In the Old Testament pagan religions, the conduct of the people was greatly influenced by the kind of god they sought to worship. If one sees God as a missionary, concerned, loving, forgiving and sacrificial, he will seek to have those traits. A greater understanding of God's nature is essential in finding out how one should be a part of His eternal purpose.

2. God Desires Fellowship With Creation

Since man is made in the image of God (Genesis 1:26), God desires fellowship with the crowning act of His creation. The fellowship God intended with His creation was broken because of sin.

> Behold, the Lord's hand is not so short that it cannot save; neither is His ear so dull that it cannot hear. But your iniquities have made a separation between you and your God (Isaiah 59:1-2).

It is God's desire that we be near Him and know Him.

> *Draw near to God* and He will draw near to you, Cleanse your hands, you sinners; and purify your hearts, you double-minded (James 4:8).

> Cease striving and *know that I am God;* I will be exalted among the nations, I will be exalted in the earth (Psalm 46:10).

When you look at the Old Testament what do you see? Because the Old Testament contains so much history, it is easy to get caught up in learning facts and names without really understanding the thrust of the Old Testament. The Old Testament is a revelation of God. If you study the Old Testament and only learn who did what and when, you have missed the main purpose for this revelation. The Old Testament tells us what God is like. The acts of God reveal to us the nature of God. The character of God is projected by what He does.

One of the central ideas revealed about God in the Old Testament

---

[1]Jim Woodroof, *The Aroma of Christ.* (Dallas, Texas: Gospel Teachers Publications, Inc., 1981), p. 45.

4

is His desire to be near His people. From the very beginning God knew that man needed companionship.

> Then the Lord God said, 'It is not good for the man to be alone; I will make him a helper suitable for him' (Genesis 2:18).

After man made the decision to transgress the will of God, we find God in the garden with His creation.

> And they heard the sound of the Lord God walking in the garden in the cool of the day, and the man and his wife hid themselves from the presence of the Lord God among the trees of the garden (Genesis 3:8).

The book of Genesis closes with the beautiful story of Joseph and the difficult times he faced. It is clear in this story that God was with him. When Joseph was sold into slavery and everything looked bad, God desired to be with him.

> *And the Lord was with Joseph,* so he became a successful man. And he was in the house of his master, the Egyptian (Genesis 39:2).

When he refused to commit immorality to avoid sinning against his God (Genesis 39:9), he was thrown into jail. However, he felt the presence of God in his life.

> *But the Lord was with Joseph* and extended kindness to him, and gave him favor in the sight of the chief jailer (Genesis 39:21). (See also Genesis 39:23.)

The revelation of the Old Testament concerning God's desire to be with His people is extended in Exodus. Not long after leaving Egypt, God commanded the tabernacle to be built. The purpose of this command is clear.

> And let them construct a sanctuary for Me, that *I may dwell among them* (Exodus 25:8).

The building of the tabernacle was a forerunner of the temple to be built under the reign of Solomon. Solomon declared that the temple was to be God's dwelling place.

> I have surely built Thee a lofty house, *A place for Thy dwelling* forever (1 Kings 8:13).

However, even at the dedication of the temple, Solomon realized that a physical building could not contain the God of the heavens.

> But will God indeed dwell on the earth? Behold, heaven
> and the highest heaven cannot contain Thee, how much
> less this house which I have built! (1 Kings 8:27).

Jesus' coming into the world was a further declaration of the desire of God to be with His people. When John states that the Word became flesh and dwelt among people (John 1:14), the word "dwelt" literally means that He "tabernacled" among people. The dwelling of God among His people is further developed in the New Testament in the concept of the church. The church as a collective group of people is referred to as the "temple of God."

> If any man destroys the temple of God, God will destroy
> him, for the *temple of God* is holy, and that is what *you
> are* (1 Corinthians 3:17).

However, not only is the collective group referred to as the temple of God, but also individuals who make up the church become the temple of the Holy Spirit which we have from God.

> Or do you not know that *your body is a temple of the Ho-
> ly Spirit* who is in you, whom *you have from God*, and
> that you are not your own? (1 Corinthians 6:19).

Not only are we as the church a temple of the Holy Spirit which is from God, but we as members of God's family are a growing temple in the Lord.

> So then you are no longer strangers and aliens, but you
> are fellow citizens with the saints, and are of God's
> household, having been built upon the foundation of the
> apostles and prophets, Christ Jesus Himself being the cor-
> ner stone, in whom the whole building, being fitted
> together is growing into a *holy temple in the Lord* (Ephe-
> sians 2:19-21).

The presence of God among his people becomes even more personalized in the New Testament than it was in the Old Testament. The New Testament makes it clear concerning the ability of God in reference to our thinking.

> Now to Him who is able to do exceeding abundantly
> beyond all that we ask or think, according to the power
> that works within us (Ephesians 3:20).

Not only do we have the promise of God's ability, but also of his desire to work in His people.

For I am confident of this very thing, that *He who began a good work in you* will perfect it until the day of Christ Jesus (Philippians 1:6).

For it is *God who is at work in you*, both to will and to work for His good pleasure (Philippians 2:13).

The revelation of God from the beginning to the present is consistent. God is a "people God," and He desires fellowship with His people. However, in spite of His desire to be with His people, He cannot accomplish this against our wills. The fellowship that God desires with us can only be brought about by the reconciling power of Christ. God is interested in obtaining our fellowship with Him, using us as instruments to bring about the reconciliation of all men. If we duplicate the nature of God in our lives, we will be interested in the fellowship of all men with God. To be indifferent to the reconciliation of the world to God is to deny the heart of the one in whose image we have been made. The desire of all disciples to reach the untold millions with the greatest story ever told is rooted in the very nature of the God we claim to serve. When you see clearly the nature of your Father, you will have to reflect what you see.

3. Sent Jesus

God's desire for fellowship with the world which is made in His image becomes clear when the price of this reconciliation becomes evident. The plan to send His only begotten son was formed in the beginning. John states that Jesus was slain from the creation of the world (Revelation 13:8, NIV). You don't have to read very far in Genesis before God begins to tell of His purpose for the world. God tells Abram that He plans to bless all the families of the earth through him (Genesis 12:3). The promise of the coming Christ is woven throughout the Old Testament revelation. Isaiah 53 is the classic chapter which reveals what would happen to the coming Messiah.

There is no greater verse in the New Testament that explains the love of God for His creation than John 3:16.

For God so loved the world, that He gave His only begotten Son, that whoever believes in Him should not perish, but have eternal life.

This verse has probably been memorized by more people and has been preserved on more posters and plaques than any one single verse in the entire New Testament. The depth of God's love is seen in His willingness to give Christ for the unlovely and disobedient.

7

For while we were still helpless, at the right time Christ died for the ungodly. For one will hardly die for a righteous man; though perhaps for the good man someone would dare even to die. But God demonstrates His own love toward us, in that while we were yet sinners, Christ died for us (Romans 5:6-8).

All of us have someone in this world with whom we feel a closeness. Perhaps it is a son, brother, sister, mother, father, niece, nephew, or just a close friend. It is difficult to see them suffer any pain, but can you imagine the love it would take for you to voluntarily inflict pain upon them for the benefit of ungodly people when they have done nothing wrong or worthy of pain? If you can grasp that thought, you will have some idea of what went on in the mind of God in giving His only son.

There can be no true love without sacrifice. In scripture, love and sacrifice are connected.

We know love by this, that He laid down His life for us; and we ought to lay down our lives for the brethren (1 John 3:16).

There is no way man can see greater love for him by His creator other than in the giving of Jesus. It is this example of sacrificial love that God had for us which is the pattern for the disciple today. The power for loving on the part of the present day disciple is found not in the act of loving, but in the supreme example of the one we are all attempting to imitate because it is in His image we have been made.

4. God Is Faithful

The revelation of God in scripture is a testimony to His faithfulness in keeping His word. If there were anything that the people of God should have learned, it was that God would do what He promised. One of the classic promises that God kept had to be the one to Abram.

And I will make you a great nation, And I will bless you, And make your name great; And so you shall be a blessing (Genesis 12:2).

Can you imagine the magnitude of this promise to someone who had no children? The promise is clearer and more concrete when Abram is asked to count all the stars to see the numberless descendants he will have (Genesis 15:5). We have the benefit of a perspective to the promise made to Abram that he never had. We know that God was

8

faithful in this promise.

With several hundred years of Jewish history as a foundation, Joshua went forth with the belief that God would be faithful in His promises. He saw firsthand that God would fulfill what He said He would do if man would do what he was asked. God promised Joshua that He would give them land, conquer all his enemies and give them success wherever they went (Joshua 1:1-7). The book of Joshua is a testimony to the faithfulness of God. God fulfilled in a mighty way everything He said He would do.

However, it seems that the faithfulness of God became clouded in the minds of the Israelites. It appears that each new generation needed to have the faithfulness of God reaffirmed. The prophets had the faithfulness of God as the heart of their message.

> 'Bring the whole tithe into the storehouse, so that there may be food in My house, and test Me now in this,' says the Lord of hosts, 'if I will not open for you the windows of heaven, and pour out for you a blessing until it overflows' (Malachi 3:10).

God is saying through Malachi what He would do if put to the test.

In a day when a "man's word" is not as good as it used to be, the faithfulness of God shines forth. The book of Hebrews helps us to further understand His faithfulness and fidelity.

> In order that by two unchangeable things, in which *it is impossible for God to lie*, we may have strong encouragement, we who have fled for refuge in laying hold of the hope set before us (Hebrews 6:18).

> Let your character be free from the love of money, being content with what you have; for He Himself has said; 'I will never desert you, nor will I ever forsake you' (Hebrews 13:5).

God is showing us the type of person He wants us to be. He wants us to be faithful to our word. God has been faithful to His word in spite of adversity and difficulty. If we are covenant and promise breakers, we are not reflecting the image of the one who made us.

Chapter 2

Manifested in Jesus

God wants His creation to be like Him, but how is this to be accomplished? How can humans be like something they have not perceived with their empirical senses (touch, taste, sight, hear and smell)? Man tends to imitate what he experiences.

The advent of Jesus solved God's need for a visual aid for His creation. As soon as Jesus came, He was declared to be Immanuel (Matthew 1:23) which means "God with us." John stated that the "Word became flesh and dwelt among us" (John 1:14). John understood that the problem was that no one had seen God, but Jesus explained God (John 1:18). When the disciples wanted to see the Father, Jesus declared that they could see the Father through Him.

> Jesus said to him, 'Have I been so long with you, and yet you have not come to know Me, Philip? *He who has seen Me has seen the Father;* how do you say, show us the Father?' (John 14:9).

In the first two chapters of Colossians we see Jesus revealed as the center of relationships. The preeminence of Jesus is set forth by showing the various relationships He sustained. In relationship to the Father, He is the image of the invisible God (1:15). In relationship to the universe, He is creator, sustainer and goal (1:16-17). In relationship to the body, the church (1:22-23), He is the head (1:18a). In relationship to the dead, He is the firstborn (1:18b). In relationship to the fulness, it all dwells in Him (1:19). In relationship to the man in sin, He is the reconciler (1:20-24). In relationship to the mystery, He is the fulfillment (1:25-29). In relationship to the treasures of wisdom and knowledge, they are all in Him (2:1-3). Paul summarized his exaltation of Jesus in 2:9:

For in Him all the fulness of Deity dwells in bodily form.

As one views Jesus he is not looking at some inferior creation, but he is viewing one in whom all the fulness of Deity dwells and who is in the image of the invisible God. The word "image" carries with it the idea of replica. In New Testament times people did not carry various charge cards or a driver's license with one's picture on it. How would they prove who they were to someone? Sometimes a description of a person was given and the bearer of the description had to match that description. The Greeks used a word for this means of identification which was similar to the word "image." In the case of Jesus, He was the description of the Father. It is true that Jesus was like God, but also God was like Jesus.

The purpose of the revelation of God in the Old Testament is to get His people to be like Him (Leviticus 11:44; 1 Peter 1:15). How can you be holy as He is holy and adopt the image of God? By duplicating in your life the only real example of how God would live on earth in a fleshly body, Jesus. In order to be like God, we will have to be like Jesus. In order to be like Jesus, we must be willing to love, to do, to hate, to accomplish what Jesus loved, did, hated and accomplished.

1. Committed to Follow God

The allegiance Jesus had to His Father was very clear. Jesus' food was to do the will of the Father and to complete His work (John 4:34). It is evident that Jesus did not pursue His own will, but the will of the one who sent Him (John 5:30). His purpose for coming from heaven to earth was to do the Father's will (John 6:38). The consistency in following His Father is seen when Jesus said He *always* did the things pleasing to His Father (John 8:29).

The great "I Am" was the center of His direction. The example of a commitment to follow God was evident. One did not have to be around Jesus for long without realizing the important part the Father played in His life.

In order to be like Jesus, who is in the image of the Father, you must do more than just doing what He did. The basis for what Jesus did was His preoccupation with the Father's will. Unless you are dominated with the overwhelming desire to do everything the Father desires of your life, you will not have a basis for true discipleship. Allowing God to completely dominate your life and thinking will turn your "oughts" into your "wants." Rules and regulations can change your behavior, but only God can change your desires.

2. Saw the World as a Mission Field

Jesus had a concern for the world that needed to be reconciled to His Father. He knew that the purpose of His coming was to save the world.

> And she will bear a Son; and you shall call His name Jesus, for it is He who will *save His people* from their sins (Matthew 1:21).

> For the Son of Man has come to seek and to *save that which is lost* (Luke 19:10).

As Jesus observed people, He saw them as a potential harvest of souls. Jesus saw that people were ready to be reached.

> Do you not say, 'There are yet four months, and then comes the harvest'? Behold, I say to you, lift up your eyes, and look on the fields that they are *white for harvest* (John 4:35).

Jesus stressed that the harvest was there, but the problem was workers (Matthew 9:37-38). Jesus saw His mission as one of preaching.

> And He said to them, 'Let us go somewhere else to the towns nearby, in order that I may preach there also; for that is what I came out for (Mark 1:38).

As a disciple of Jesus you must begin to see what Jesus saw. When you see large crowds at an athletic contest, what do you see? If Jesus were watching the thousands at the Super Bowl, what do you believe His thoughts and chief concerns would be? Do you believe His thoughts would be centered on which team is ahead or how much time is left in the game? To ask these questions is to answer them. The next time you find yourself surrounded by thousands, ask yourself, "Is this the harvest?" The heart of Jesus was so in tune with the Father that He could look on the crowds and have compassion. Until we can look on crowds and see them as sheep without a shepherd, we have not developed the sight of Jesus.

The last words of anyone prior to his leaving his friends reflect the most serious concerns of his heart. Jesus is not an exception to this observation. As recorded in Mark 16:15-16 and Matthew 28:18-20, Jesus made it clear that He wanted His message to go to all the nations in the world. This great commission was not intended to give the disciples some busy work, but to develop in them the heart of the Father reflected in the life of Jesus. If the disciples of Jesus are to imitate the Father (Ephesians 5:1), they must have the same interests and concerns the Father has.

The deep concern that Jesus had in doing the will of the Father has been previously established. Jesus stated that the will of the Father involved people believing in Jesus which would result in eternal life.

> For this is the will of My Father, that everyone who

beholds the Son and believes in Him, may have eternal life; and I Myself will raise him up on the last day (John 6:40).

3. Counted the Cost

As the Father knew the reconciliation of the world to himself (2 Corinthians 5:19) was not going to be cheap, Jesus also knew that His work for the Father was not going to be accomplished without a high price being paid.

For even the Son of Man did not come to be served, but to serve and *to give His life* a ransom for many (Mark 10:45).

Peter made it clear concerning the price of redemption when he said it was not paid with silver or gold, but by the unblemished lamb (1 Peter 1:18-19).

Paul discussed the cost of Jesus in the scheme of redemption (Philippians 2:5-11). Jesus existed in the form of God which meant He possessed the same nature. "Form" is not synonymous with material shape, but it has to do with essential nature. The equality of God was established; however, it was not something that was to be held on to at all cost. The word for "grasped" means to be held on to at all cost, as a plunderer would hold on to his prize. Because of the need to redeem the world, Jesus was willing to pay the price of giving up His right to deity.

The cost of the sacrifice of Jesus is further discussed when Paul said that Jesus emptied Himself. Jesus emptied Himself of the outward expression of deity because His advent was in the form of a servant which was not deity. He emptied Himself as an equal with God and surrendered His omnipresence. Jesus became a man in order to die because God in his unaltered essence cannot die. Jesus was made like His brethren (Hebrews 2:17-18) and exposed Himself to the temptations of man (Hebrews 4:14-16). The cost of Jesus could be summarized by stating that He emptied Himself, became a human in a sinless body, used the body as a servant and willingly died on the cross. Jesus was able to identify with the outcasts of society where the suffering was real.

In the context of Philippians 2, Paul immediately follows the supreme example of Jesus in His willingness to empty Himself with two examples of his fellow laborers who had done the same. The sacrificial nature of Jesus is given as an example for us to follow.

The first example Paul gives is Timothy. Timothy was genuinely

13

concerned about the welfare of the Philippians (Philippians 2:20). Paul adds that he was a willing servant of others.

> But you know of his proven worth that he served with me in the futherance of the gospel like a child serving his father (Philippians 2:22).

This kind and compassionate young servant is an extension of the Lord he had accepted as the King of his life.

Paul's second example was Epaphroditus. This great servant was willing to do what had to be done for the cause in which he believed.

> Therefore receive him in the Lord with all joy, and hold men like him in high regard; because he came close to death for the work of Christ, *risking his life* to complete what was deficient in your service to me (Philippians 2:29-30).

His willingness to risk his life can only be traced back to the great example of Christ.

With Christ as the ultimate example of self-sacrifice, followed by two examples duplicating the same pattern in their own ministries, the modern disciple is left with no choice in his own personal life. As our teacher, Jesus is not leaving us with an option as to whether our following will be inexpensive. You cannot be pleased with your following of Jesus if all it involves is attending a few events each week as a passive spectator. The general religious world believes that following Jesus does not demand as radical a price in the 20th century as it did in the first century. The first century church was able to be successful because of the unanimous choice to pay the price of discipleship. When the religious community of the 20th century gets serious about following a sacrificial leader, first century results will be seen in this century.

4. Finished the Task

Jesus knew that He had a great task ahead of Him and He needed to be diligent in completing it.

> We must work the works of Him who sent Me, as long as it is day; night is coming when no man can work (John 9:4).

As He came to the closing moment on the cross, He realized He had completed the task when He said, "It is finished" (John 19:30). He came into the world to save sinners and to purchase the church.

14

It is a trustworthy statement, deserving full acceptance, that Christ Jesus came into the world to *save sinners*, among whom I am foremost of all (1 Timothy 1:15).

Be on guard for yourselves and for all the flock, among which the Holy Spirit has made you overseers, to shepherd the *church of God which He purchased with His own blood* (Acts 20:28).

Husbands, love your wives, just as Christ also loved the church and *gave Himself up for her* (Ephesians 5:25).

Peter's sermon described how Jesus followed the purpose of God and completed everything He set forth to accomplish (Acts 2:22-36).

Jesus fulfilled the typology of the Old Testament as discussed in Hebrews 9:11-12. He entered the greater and more perfect tabernacle with a sacrifice of Himself which will never have to be repeated. The Old Testament sacrifices always looked forward to the "once for all" nature of the sacrifice of Jesus. This was part of the purpose that God had had for His Son from the beginning.

And all who dwell on the earth will worship him, everyone whose name has not been written from the foundation of the world in the book of life of the Lamb who has been slain (Revelation 13:8).

Conclusion

The design that our creator has for our lives as disciples should be clearer after a brief study of the nature of God (in which discipleship is rooted) and its manifestation in Jesus. God manifested in Jesus the design that He had for the crowning act of His creation. You are urged to see the strong correlation between the Father and the Son as the design of discipleship. The following chart will show the relationship as the foundation for God's children:

God		Christ	
1.	I am	1.	Committed to follow God
2.	Desires fellowship with creation	2.	Saw world as a mission field
3.	Sent Jesus	3.	Counted the cost
4.	Is faithful	4.	Finished the task

If you believe you have been created in His image and you understand that the basic purpose of conversion is to become like Him, the portrayal of your discipleship should be clearer to you. The extension of the nature of God as manifested in Jesus makes it even clearer what you should be. Jesus was not free to do as He pleased as a replica of the Father and neither do you have the choice to do as you please as a follower of Jesus. As you behold the Son, the pattern for your life is established. All of life must be measured in respect to how it reflects the glory of God. It was for this end we were brought into the world. If God is not being shown and glorified in His crowning creation, man is not reflecting His Father or fulfilling the eternal purpose for his existence.

Section II

Demand of Discipleship

Since the church is central in the eternal purpose of God, the life style of those who comprise the "called out" of God is also essential in this great purpose. Since the church is not made up of material things such as wood or stone, the purpose of God really finds its fulfillment in the people who are the church.

Jesus' real purpose of life revealed itself in the demands He placed upon His followers. Jesus followed a very important principle of leadership in that He would not ask others to be what He was not. He would not ask them to go where He would not go. Jesus was a pace setter in every aspect of His life, whether it was sacrifice, endurance, faithfulness, compassion, courage or determination. As the ministry of Jesus unfolded, it became increasingly clear that He was calling His disciples or pupils to be like Him.

> A pupil is not above his teacher; but everyone, after he has been fully trained *will be like his teacher* (Luke 6:40).

The essential nature of the ministry of Christ was calling people to be like Him. This is further developed by the disciples of Jesus.

> The one who says he abides in Him ought himself to walk in the same manner *as He walked* (1 John 2:6).

> For you have been called for this purpose, since Christ also suffered for you, leaving you an *example for you to follow* in His steps (1 Peter 2:21).

> Have this attitude in yourselves which was also in Christ Jesus (Philippians 2:5).

> My children, with whom I am again in labor until *Christ is formed in you* (Galatians 4:19).

In this section a pattern is developed using scriptures found in the

17

four gospels which demonstrate the demand of discipleship as an extension of the manifested life of Jesus who is the image of the Father. This pattern is: (1) a commitment to Jesus, (2) a desire and preparation to reach the world, (3) a price to be paid, (4) a faithfulness in following.

Chapter 3

Mark 1:17-20

> And Jesus said to them, 'Follow me, and I will make you become fishers of men.' And they immediately left the nets and followed Him. And going on a little farther, He saw James, the son of Zebedee, and John his brother, who were also in the boat mending nets. And immediately He called them; and they left their father Zebedee in the boat with the hired servants, and went away to follow Him.

As Mark set forth his description and account of Jesus' life, it was not long until Jesus called people to follow Him. Mark's account of the life of Jesus centered around, and elaborated more on, the nature of discipleship than did the other accounts. Each account has a little different flavor of the life of Jesus. Because His life was unique, it is hard to give a complete picture of everything about Him.

Sometimes the Biblical student loses something when he tries to compare and harmonize the 'four accounts of Jesus' life. Great benefits can come from comparing accounts, but one might lose the thrust of the writer by constant comparison. If one views each account as a portrait of Jesus without attempting to put all the portaits in one picture, the stress of a particular writer will be seen with greater ease.

Jesus finds the disciples working as fishermen on the shores of the Sea of Galilee. (Other names are the Sea of Tiberias and the Lake of Gennesaret.) The place where they were fishing was considered the "hot spot" for first century fishermen. Various kinds of fish were caught here that were not found in other places. This call of Jesus to discipleship was marked with urgency and challenge and the disciples responded in a similar manner. This challenge was going to demand a break with the ties of their occupation in order to accept a greater challenge.

You can begin reading in any account of the life of Jesus and see that He is a challenging Savior. You cannot simply view Jesus as a great teacher because the nature of His teaching demands an evaluation on your part. You cannot take a realistic look at Jesus and go away the same individual. The ability of Jesus to quickly challenge the first century fishermen to discipleship is still available today. As you look at the passages which show the demand of discipleship placed on the people of the first century, you must make some evaluations of your own concerning your life. The accounts of Jesus are not to be read as you would the history of World War II. You can read a history book and make intellectual conclusions that have nothing to do with your daily conduct as an individual, but reading the account of Jesus is different.

1. Follow Me

The call of Jesus for others to follow Him became the battle cry of His ministry. Every account of the life of Jesus carries abundant evidence of this truth (Matthew 4:19; 8:22; 9:9; 19:21; Mark 2:14; 8:34; 10:21; Luke 5:27; 9:23; 9:59; John 12:26; 21:19). The idea of following is not new. God explained that the Israelites who came up out of Egypt were not allowed to see the promised land because they did not follow God fully.

> None of the men came up from Egypt, from twenty years old and upward, shall see the land which I swore to Abraham, to Isaac and to Jacob; for *they did not follow Me fully* (Numbers 32:11).

The follower of Jesus is not given the luxury of choosing his own pathway to the Father. He is demanded to follow Jesus. Following Jesus is important if you want to find the Father. As you study Mark, it becomes clear that Jesus is not the central figure, but God is. Jesus is the way to God.

> Jesus said to him 'I am the way, and the truth, and the life, no one comes to the Father, but through Me' (John 14:6).

If you will follow Jesus, you will find the Father because that is where Jesus is going.

> Jesus, knowing that the Father had given all things into His hands, and that He had come forth from God, and *was going back to God* (John 13:3).

19

And concerning righteousness, because *I go to the Father*, and you no longer behold Me (John 16:10).

The parting words of Jesus stated that He was going to the Father.

And Jesus, crying out with a loud voice, said, '*Father, into Thy hands I commit My spirit.*' And having said this, He breathed His last (Luke 23:46).

Jesus is not the end of the journey for the disciple, but He is the means to the end. He is essential if you are to reach the Father.

Jesus is the focal point of your discipleship. In the case of Joseph of Arimathea, Matthew said he was discipled to Jesus.

And when it was evening, there came a rich man from Arimathea, named Joseph, who himself had also become a disciple of Jesus (Matthew 27:57).

The Greek word for disciple in 27:57 is a verb (aorist passive) and not a noun. The grammar would communicate the idea that either Joseph was discipled to Jesus as the object of his discipleship, or he was discipled to Jesus as the instrument or means of discipleship. It is possible for this verse to communicate both of these ideas. If in other places Jesus can occupy two parts in the same figure (in the figure of the building, Jesus is both foundation and cornerstone, 1 Corinthians 3:11; Ephesians 2:20), He can be both the object of your discipleship and the means by which you are discipled. Jesus as the object of the disciple's allegiance is stressed in later writings. Lydia realized her faithfulness was to the Lord.

And when she and her household had been baptized, she urged us, saying, 'If you have judged me to be faithful *to the Lord*, come into my house and stay." And she prevailed upon us (Acts 16:15).

Barnabas urged the young church in Antioch to be faithful to Jesus.

then when he had come and witnessed the grace of God, he rejoiced and began to encourage them all with resolute heart to remain true *to the Lord* (Acts 11:23).

The secret to sacrificial giving is attributed to one's allegiance to the Lord.

And this, not as we had expected, but they first gave themselves *to the Lord* and to us by the will of God (2 Corinthians 8:5).

20

2. Become Fishers of Men

The great heart of God that desires fellowship with His creation and the great compassion of Jesus for the fields that are ready for harvest surfaced in the immediate challenge "to follow" and "to become fishers of men." This part of the challenge to discipleship is a concrete extension of the ministry of Jesus and the eternal purpose of God. The eternal purpose of God in Ephesians included making the Gentiles to be fellow heirs, fellow members and "fellow partakers of the promise in Christ through the gospel" (Ephesians 3:6).

It needs to be remembered that Jesus was calling others to be what He was, i.e. fisher of men. It is interesting to note that in the Old Testament God is depicted as a fisher of men. The Old Testament passages which show this are usually stressing some type of divine judgment.

> 'Behold, I am going to send for many fishermen,' declares the Lord, 'and they will fish for them; and afterwards I shall send for many hunters, and they will hunt them from every mountain and every hill, and from the clefts of the rocks (Jeremiah 16:16).

> And I will turn you about, and put hooks into your jaws. . . (Ezekiel 38:4).

> The Lord God has sworn by His holiness, 'Behold the days are coming upon you when they will take you away with meat hooks, And the last of you with fish hooks' (Amos 4:2).

Therefore depicting the disciples as fishermen was an extension of the work of God in the Old Testament. Jesus is going to make "catchers of men" out of disciples in order to make people ready for the judgment day. It will be the disciple's task to catch the fish and God's to decide their fate.

> Again, the kindness of heaven is like a dragnet cast into the sea, and gathering fish of every kind; and when it was filled, they drew it up on the beach; and they sat down, and gathered the good fish into containers, but the bad they threw away. So it will be at the end of the age; the angels shall come forth, and take out the wicked from among the righteous, and will cast them into the furnace of fire; there shall be weeping and gnashing of teeth (Matthew 13:47-50).

As the disciples experienced their close fellowship with Jesus, it was natural for them to become fishers of men. You tend to become like those you are around (Luke 6:40). Their becoming fishers of men was not something done by their own power. Jesus said, "I will make you become fishers of men."

Paul discussed how disciples are really made in his manual on ministry—the book of 2 Corinthians. In 3:18 he said we "are being transformed into the same image" as we behold the glory of the Lord with an unveiled face. The word for transformed is a passive verb which communicates something is being done to us and not by us. Instead of being the agent or the means for transformation into His likeness, you serve as the object of that transformation. The means of the transformation of the earlier disciples was that of beholding Jesus.

> And the Word became flesh, and dwelt among us, and *we beheld His glory*, glory as the only begotten from the Father, full of grace and truth (John 1:14).

> For we did not follow cleverly devised tales when we made known to you the power and coming of our Lord Jesus Christ, but *we were eyewitnesses of His majesty* (2 Peter 1:16).

The transformation by means of beholding produced a God-made man rather than a self-made man.

Paul was strong on the idea of man's dependency on God for help rather than on man's own means and methods. He declared that your adequacy is from God, not yourself.

> Not that we are adequate in ourselves to consider anything as coming from ourselves, but *our adequacy is from God* (2 Corinthians 3:5).

Your trust is not to be in yourself (2 Corinthians 1:9) because you are His workmanship (Ephesians 2:10) led to His triumph (2 Corinthians 2:14). Changing the disciples of Jesus into the image of Christ took place over a period of time. At times the disciples were not even aware that these changes in thought, attitude and direction took place. The "sandy" Peter did not become the rock, and the impatient John (Luke 9:54) did not become the servant (Revelation 1:1), without spending some time beholding Jesus.

As soon as the challenge of Jesus was received and acted upon, Jesus proceeded to do what He had called them to do—reach men! One of the first acts these early disciples were to "behold" was Jesus teaching (Mark 1:21). Training for the ministry of Christ began as soon as they were called to discipleship.

It is not unusual for followers to receive their motivation for achievement from their leader. For years the Green Bay Packers were the champions of the football world. They were a team feared by their opponents, loved by their fans and lauded in the record books. The real secret to their success could be traced to their coach, Vince Lombardi. Everyone wanted to win for the coach. Their inspiration to put forth effort was more inspired from the bench than from the bleachers. Similarly, Jesus provided the example and motivation for the early disciples to succeed. As their love for Christ developed, so did their keen desire to please Him. When disciples determine to practice the presence of Jesus (Hebrews 4:13) and with determination "play" to the throne rather than to the throng, the world will know the message of Jesus. The disciple must cease seeking the approval of men (Galatians 1:10) and seek the approval of God (2 Timothy 3:15). The disciple must desire the applause of heaven rather than cater to the fashions and whims of the world from which he has been transformed (Romans 12:1-2).

Jesus related His mission for the world and His specific mission for His disciples in a way that they could best understand—through fishing. It is not clear whether the disciples understood all the implications of what it meant to be fishers of men as followers of Christ, but in time they did learn. Jesus began His demand to follow with a concept they could at least relate to. Fishing, an occupation for many of the disciples of Jesus, had both its rewards and difficulties. The occupation of fishing, which brought both victories and defeats, was one that prepared the disciples for both the good days and the bad days ahead.

3. Leave Occupation

The disciples willingly left one of their greatest securities—their nets (Mark 1:18). There is no discipleship without some type of sacrifice. The eternal purpose of God for His creation was not without the price of His only Son. For Jesus to call people into a discipleship without a price would have produced a following without any great loyalty because there had been no price paid.

To leave nets to follow Jesus might not seem too expensive to you. In our modern day, for most people, fishing is recreation or a hobby, and they are not dependent upon their success for their livelihood. In fact, if the fishermen I know were to calculate what the fish they catch cost per pound when all their expenses of fishing are totaled, they could buy their fish at half price at the local fish store! Fishing was not recreation to the early disciples, but their main source of income. Even though it was an unpredictable source of income, it was what they had been trained by their fathers to do. After leaving this source of revenue, they didn't know if they could return to their own equipment. There is no indication that they had stored up a large amount of cash to tide them over as they learned to be fishers of men. Their determination to follow Jesus carried with it a great degree of uncertainty. To get a feel for the cost they were willing to pay, what would it take for you to walk away from your job without the promise of a comparable salary in return? A man usually does not change jobs unless he feels he can better himself. These early disciples were willing to pay a great price without even knowing where the next meal was coming from or what the future held for them.

This high cost of discipleship is continually seen in the teachings of Jesus. When Jesus likens the kingdom of heaven to one who finds a pearl, He shows the great cost one is willing to pay.

> Again, the kingdom of heaven is like a merchant seeking fine pearls, and upon finding one pearl of great value, he went and *sold all that he had*, and bought it (Matthew 13:45-46).

The challenge to a certain ruler was basically the same.

> And when Jesus heard this, He said to him, 'One thing you still lack; *sell all that you possess*, and distribute it to the poor, and you shall have treasure in heaven; and come, follow Me' (Luke 18:22).

The price may vary from individual to individual and from generation to generation, but it is, nevertheless, all that you have. This type of demand does not fit well in our security conscious age, but how else is the demand of Jesus to be interpreted? There is no cheap way to follow Jesus.

4. Followed Jesus

Mark's conclusion of this first call to discipleship was that they followed Him (1:18). When others were called, the same conclusion was expressed (1:20). They did not know where the decision to follow Jesus would lead, but they began by a faithful and simple following of the man from Nazareth. Their Jewish nationalistic ideas might have led them to believe that they would be involved in a great battle with the military forces of Rome, but Jesus was going to spend some time in the remainder of His ministry correcting their erroneous idea of what it meant to follow the Messiah.

As they left their nets, boats, family and friends, what did following Jesus entail? The initial challenge to follow Jesus involved the disciples in learning from Jesus and watching Him deal with the situations of life. The first action of Jesus is shocking to these new disciples. He casts the unclean spirit out of a man (Mark 1:23-28). This great miracle caused some of the disciples to be amazed and to ask, "What is this?" This was just the beginning of a series of miracles that left the disciples with the truth that their leader could handle any problem. However, in spite of the great success of His healing ministry over the demon-possessed, lepers, and crippled, the disciples saw the real mission of fishermen. Jesus allowed them to see that the mission which He was engaged in could not be accomplished without communication with the Father.

> And in the early morning, while it was still dark, He arose and went out and departed to a lonely place, and was praying there (Mark 1:35).

After the disciples had found Him, He reiterated the purpose for His coming and their calling.

> And He said to them, 'Let us go somewhere else to the towns nearby, in order that I may preach there also; for that is what I came out for' (Mark 1:38).

This incident was going to serve the disciples as a model for their own personal ministry in the years to come.

The transformation of the minds of the disciples to be in tune with the mind of Jesus is vividly demonstrated in the situation where they find themselves in Acts 6. The early evangelistic efforts of the church were marked with great success, but there arose a group who felt their needs were not being met. It would have been a real temptation of the apostles to reason that such successful efforts would merit taking time out from their evangelistic activities to meet the physical needs of this group, but because they were so possessed with the mind of Christ, they responded as men "who had been with Jesus" (Acts 4:13).

> And the twelve summoned the congregation of the disciples and said, 'It is not desirable for us to neglect the word of God in order to serve tables. But select from among you, brethren, seven men of good reputation, full

of the Spirit and of wisdom, whom we may put in charge of this task. But we will devote ourselves to prayer, and to the ministry of the word' (Acts 6:2-4).

This concrete example of the actions of the apostles shows that following Jesus involves more than watching and learning, but incorporating the mind of Jesus into the mind of the disciple.

The kind of following that Jesus demands of us today is similar. Jesus is not desiring to create robots with a few regulations, but disciples who are changed because they "beheld." Learning all the stories and events in the life of Jesus without a change in our own minds is to make a farce of following Jesus. The account of Jesus was not given so we could edit a few regulations from them, but to reveal the life of Jesus so we could see the standard for our existence. A simple intellectual approach to the facts of the life of Jesus without some type of internalizing is not getting to the root of what it means to follow Him. Even in these early days of following Him, the disciples did not understand everything they heard or know how to implement everything He did into their lives. This initial beginning to follow in Mark 1:17-18 was a simple one, but it was a beginning. If you are serious about being His disciple, you must be willing to start now. Fear of not being able to finish is not a justifiable excuse not to begin. Did you ever finish anything you did not start? Of course not! Neither will you ever finish the course in the school of discipleship unless you begin.

Chapter 4

Mark 8:34-38

And He summoned the multitude with His disciples, and said to them, 'If anyone wishes to come after Me, let him deny himself, and take up his cross, and follow Me. For whoever wishes to save his life shall lose it; but whoever loses his life for My sake and the gospel's shall save it. For what does it profit a man to gain the whole world, and forfeit his soul? For what shall a man give in exchange for his soul? For whoever is ashamed of Me and My words in this adulterous and sinful generation, the Son of Man will also be ashamed of him when He comes in the glory of His Father with the holy angels.

Some time had passed since Jesus gave the first challenge to follow Him. During this time the disciples had a chance to watch Jesus and to behold the One they were to imitate. Jesus appointed the twelve to be with Him before He sent them out to preach (Mark 3:14). After training the twelve, He sent them out to preach (Mark 6:7-12). They preached extensively throughout the north country of Galilee. Jesus gathered them together for a report on what they had learned on the preaching tour. As He went "with His disciples to the villages of Caesarea Philippi" (Mark 8:27). He asked them who *people* thought He was. (This phrase "with His disciples" appears many times in the gospel accounts: Matthew 9:10; Mark 2:15; Luke 7:11; 8:22; 9:18; John 3:22; 6:3; 18:1.) After many answers were given, He asked who *they* thought He was. Peter was able to give the right answer:

> And He continued by questioning them, 'But who do you say that I am?" Peter answered and said to Him, *'Thou art the Christ'* (Mark 8:29).

Jesus instructed Peter to tell no one, because in spite of giving the right answer, he had the wrong concept of the Christ. Imagine the disappointment of Peter. He had been following Jesus for a couple of years and had become the one with all the wrong answers or inappropriate statements. For a change, he had given the right answer before all the other disciples. Before he could feel good about his right answer, he was told to tell no one.

As usual, Jesus knew Peter better than Peter knew himself because immediately Jesus predicted His death and resurrection three days later. Seemingly without drawing a breath, Peter began telling Jesus how this could never be. Why did Peter think this should never be true of Jesus? Peter already had his mind made up how the Messiah should conduct himself. Dying and being raised was not part of the plan Peter had for the Messiah. In addition to the prediction of His death and resurrection three days later in Mark 8:31, Jesus repeats the same teaching in nearly the same words twice more (Mark 9:31; 10:33-34). Had the disciples understood the teachings of Jesus, where would they have been three days after His death? An open-minded disciple who accepted everything Jesus said about Himself would have been at the entrance of the tomb waiting for Him to come forth. They were not there! Even when the disciples were informed of His resurrection by the women, they did not believe it (Mark 16:11). It is interesting that the young man (we presume he was an angel) at the tomb instructed the women to go and tell the disciples and Peter about the resurrection. There appears to be an emphasis on Peter knowing this truth. This might be explained in light of his gross misunderstanding.

We can condemn Peter for his shallowness and unwillingness to accept the Messiah for who He was, but we can be guilty of the same mistake. Listening to the teachings of Jesus with an open mind is not an easy task for any disciple. We can be guilty of taking the teachings of Jesus, filtering them through 2000 years of Christendom, and coming out with a Messiah that is just as foreign to the truth as the one Peter had created in his own mind. The answer to this problem is the same answer God was trying to get the disciples to see in the first century. When God spoke to the disciples on the mount of transfiguration, He gave the answer to the problem: "This is my beloved Son, listen to Him!" (Mark 9:7). The disciple must learn the art of listening for the purpose of learning and not for confirmation of what he already believes is true.

We tend to hear only what we want to, and to filter out anything we do not want to hear. The problem in the communication of Jesus was not in what He said, but how we receive or interpret what He said. This is an age old problem of communication which can be illustrated with this story. "A lady was considering a divorce and sought a preacher for counsel. The preacher asked whether or not she had 'grounds' for this divorce. She replied she had 'three acres.' The preacher, realizing she didn't understand the first question, continued his counseling by asking if her husband had a 'grudge.' After some thought the lady responded, 'No, but he has a carport.' Trying again, the preacher asked if he ever 'beat her up.' She quickly responded by saying, 'Oh no! I always get up before he does in the morning!' At this point the preacher decided to let her tell him why she wanted the divorce. She replied, 'Preacher, you might find this hard to believe, but my husband and I can't carry on a decent conversation anymore!' "

The challenge for us in the discipleship demands of Jesus is to hear them as they are and not how we would wish them to be.

1. Must Desire to Follow Jesus

Jesus is quite disturbed with Peter's faulty understanding of the work of the Messiah. He assumed some of the other disciples had the same problem. Surely the multitude needed some instruction in this matter. In the challenge to follow Him, He contrasted the human direction outlined by Peter and the real direction that following must take.

> And He was stating the matter plainly. And Peter took
> Him aside and began to rebuke Him. But turning around

and seeing His disciples, He rebuked Peter, and said, 'Get behind Me, Satan; for you are not setting your mind on God's interests, but man's' (Mark 8:32-33).

Jesus' severe rebuke of Peter shows the seriousness with which Jesus took this misunderstanding. To call Peter "Satan" must have been a shock to Peter and to the rest of the apostles. Jesus quickly follows by telling Peter that he is setting his mind in the wrong direction. He is accused of being more concerned with human interests than divine interests.

By mentioning His death prior to His challenge to follow, Jesus is showing that the destiny of His life will also be the destiny of their own. Apparently this served as a base for something Peter later said to suffering Christians.

Beloved, do not be surprised at the fiery ordeal among you, which comes upon you for your testing, as though some strange thing were happening to you; but to the degree that you share the sufferings of Christ, keep on rejoicing; so that also at the revelation of His glory, you may rejoice with exultation (1 Peter 4:12-13).

To this great truth Paul adds that suffering with Christ is necessary for glorification.

And if children, heirs also, heirs of God and fellow heirs with Christ, if indeed *we suffer with Him* in order that we may also *be gloried with Him* (Romans 8:17).

The challenge to come after Christ demands a shifting of your priorities and goals. Following Jesus has always demanded adjustments on the part of followers. If you say that following Jesus has not changed your lifestyle, then you are not following the man from Nazareth, but some pseudo-20th century imitation! The abandonment of our own pathways for the will of God as expressed in Jesus will always challenge the greatest effort of man.

2. Must Deny Self and Take Up His Cross

The second part of the challenge of discipleship in Mark 1:17-20 stressed the importance of being a fisher of men. However, this part of discipleship is lacking in Mark 8:34-38, but the concept of denying self and taking up a cross are mentioned. These are missing in Mark 1:17-20. These two ideas are easily correlated by realizing men cannot be caught without serious efforts being put forth by the fishermen. The disciples knew from experience you could not be a

29

fisher of fish without some serious personal sacrifice. The same would be true with such an elusive catch as man.

When Jesus challenged the multitude and His disciples, He chose to use the imperatives: deny, take and follow. The first two imperatives, deny and take up, are aorist which usually point to action or a one-time action which is not continuous. However, when Jesus commanded them to follow, He used a present imperative which indicated that one does it continuously. There must be a point in the life of the follower where he "denies" and "takes up" as a definite decision, but the command to follow is the quest of his entire earthly following of the Christ.

Understanding what Jesus meant by "his cross" is essential in the life of the follower. Jesus did not challenge His disciples to do something that was not a part of His life. It is clear that Jesus was willing to bear His own cross for the disciples:

> They took Jesus therefore and He went out, *bearing His own cross*, to the place called the Place of a Skull, which is called in Hebrew, Golgotha (John 19:17).

The best explanation of what Jesus meant by the cross is supplied by Mark. Beginning in chapter 9 and continuing through the rest of the book, Mark spent most of the time discussing what Jesus' cross meant to Him so the disciples could get a better understanding of what it meant for them. If the pupils were to be like their teacher, they had to understand the cross.

Because of the cross, there were certain demands placed on Jesus. The cross demanded courage in the face of opposition.

> And they were seeking to seize Him; and yet they feared the multitude; for they understood that He spoke the parable against them. And so they left Him, and went away (Mark 12:12).

The cross demanded confidence and trust in a time of stress and grief.

> And He was saying, 'Abba! Father! *All things are possible for Thee;* remove this cup from Me; yet not what I will, but what Thou wilt' (Mark 14:36).

The cross demanded surrender to the will of God (14:36) at a time of discouragement over a lack of courage on the part of the disciples (14:5). The reception of unfair criticism (14:56; 15:3) and mockery (15:17-18, 29) were only surpassed by the physical abuse (14:65) and loneliness (15:34).

The mountain peak passage for what the cross really meant for Jesus—and what it should mean for the disciples—appears in Mark 14:32-39. As Jesus came into this house, He was distressed, troubled and grieved (14:33-34). The essence of His prayer was that "the hour might pass Him by" (14:35). Mark recorded the actual expression of His prayer. He called upon His Father and addressed Him as "Abba." This title denoted a real and genuine closeness. Jesus believed that there was nothing His Father could not handle: "For nothing will be impossible with God" (Luke 1:27). The ministry of Jesus was a living testimony to this truth because Jesus had seen the dead raised, the lepers made clean, the blind receive sight, the hungry fed and the crippled walk. Because of the great confidence He had in His Father, He made the request of the removal of the cup. The cup not only involved the physical death of Jesus, but it also involved the heavy weight of being the sin-bearer for the entire world. As it were in the same breath, He asked for the removal of the cup, and He expressed His willingness for the will of the Father to be done in His life. The cross for Jesus became the acceptance of the will of God for His life whether He wanted it or not, whether He understood it or not, because He was a man who was ruled by God. Therefore, the cross became for the disciples the acceptance of the will of God for their lives because in discipleship one is called to be like Him. The disciple must have the thinking of Christ to be a follower of Christ. Paul accepted the happenings in his ministry which he did not understand because he knew he must bear a similar cross, as Jesus did. Paul was willing to be a fool, to be a servant, and to endure insults, distresses, persecutions and difficulties for the sake of Christ.

> We are fools for *Christ's sake*, but you are prudent in Christ; we are weak, but you are strong; you are distinguished, but we are without honor (1 Corinthians 4:10).

> For we who live are constantly being delivered over to death *for Jesus' sake*, that the life of Jesus also may be manifested in our mortal flesh (2 Corinthians 4:11).

> Therefore I am well content with weaknesses, with insults, with distresses, with persecutions, with difficulties, for *Christ's sake;* for when I am weak, then I am strong (2 Corinthians 12:10).

When you are willing to learn self-denial and the meaning of the cross for your life, being a fisher of men will be very natural. Becoming a fisher of men without learning the meaning of the cross and self-denial is like trying to teach one to be a fisher of fish who never wanted to leave all the comforts of home and still catch fish!

Paul gives us a vivid example of this type of self-denial and cross bearing. It is also important to notice that he relates it to Jesus who is his example for all of life.

> We are afflicted in every way, but not crushed; perplexed, but not despairing; persecuted, but not forsaken; struck down, but not destroyed; always carrying about in the body the dying of Jesus, that the life of Jesus also may be manifested in our body. For we who live are constantly being delivered over to death for Jesus' sake, that the life of Jesus also may be manifested in our mortal flesh (2 Corinthians 4:8-11).

Paul realized that all of the conflicts and difficulties that Jesus faced in His life were also faced in Paul's. He did not allow these problems to keep him from his mission because he was following the example of self-denial and cross bearing that he had seen in the life of Jesus. When Paul described the apostles, he used terminology that was "cross related." Some examples of this terminology are "on display," "condemned to die," "made a spectacle," "we are fools," "we are weak" and "we are dishonored" (1 Corinthians 4:9-10, NIV).

How are self-denial and cross bearing manifested in your life? The realities of the demands of Jesus became part of the everyday lifestyle of the early disciples. If your lifestyle is no different than the lifestyle of the good, moral atheist, where is the discipleship? Accepting the will of God in an unreserved way marks the disciple as a true follower of Christ.

3. Must Lose Life to Find It

The disciples paid a price of leaving their nets (Mark 1:17-20). Jesus included a price for following which is very dear—one's life. The statement of Jesus appeared to be a paradox—if you find your life, you will lose it; and if you lose it, you will find it. The key to understanding this paradox is the little phrase in 8:35 "for my sake." This phrase gives meaning to other passages in Mark. In 10:29 Jesus declares that one would receive a hundred-fold for everything he lost if he did it for Jesus' sake. In 13:9 He told His followers they would receive opposition for Jesus' sake. There can be no real following of Jesus unless what is done is connected to Him. The follower is to endure for the sake of Christ, because He was willing to become poor for the sake of the follower.

> For you know the grace of our Lord Jesus Christ, that
> though He was rich, yet *for your sake He became poor*,
> that you through His poverty might become rich
> (2 Corinthians 8:9).

There cannot be much quality in your following Jesus without some loss or pain. In some of the weight lifting rooms in schools and colleges there is a sign which reads: "No pain; no gain." This statement is true in developing your physical strength, and it is also true in developing a strong relationship with the Father through the Son. There is also the sign, "Champions stay late." Developing a strong allegiance to Jesus is not accomplished by a few short workouts but with persistence and time.

American advertisements capitalize on the desire for people to gain much without effort by means of some "short cut." The body-building ads show a skinny man contrasted to a muscular, well-built man. The explanation gives you the impression you can have the same results in 30 days with only 60 seconds of effort a day! If it were that easy, every athletic coach in the country would use it for his team. The overweight are told of a wonder diet that allows them to eat all they want and still lose weight rapidly without exercising! These ads get thousands of responses because of their "quick result" and "no effort" promises.

The desire for discipleship in the lives of followers will not be genuine unless a price is paid. The story is told of a returning missionary who told of his great work in Africa and how God had blessed it. A woman ran up to him after his speech and declared she would give the world to be the kind of disciple that he was. The missionary responded, "That is what it cost me—the world!"

There is no greater motto for the disciple to live by than the statement of Jesus: "For what does it profit a man to gain the whole world and forfeit his soul? For what shall a man give in exchange for his soul?" As we observe discipleship in the early church as revealed in Acts, this motto was one they accepted. The disciple struggled with the conflict between the spirit and the flesh. Many times the struggle was not between the things that were clearly wrong and right, but to know what was really important. Worldliness is defined as misplaced priorities. It is easier to decide between right and wrong than it is to decide between better and best. The disciple must realize there is a price to be paid if discipleship is to be gained. The free enterprise system says "There ain't no such thing as a free lunch." Discipleship says there can be no gaining of life with the Savior without the loss of life.

4. Must Not Be Ashamed of Jesus

Following Jesus demands fidelity. Jesus stated that the disciple could not be ashamed of Jesus without Jesus' being ashamed of him when He comes again. The judgment scene in Matthew 25 established the axiom that we will be treated by Jesus the way we treat others. The disciple is expected to remain loyal until Jesus comes. When one says, "I will follow Jesus," it is not a temporary commitment. The disciple must remain loyal for life. Discipleship and faithfulness are rooted in the second-coming. Paul's motivation to Titus to live sensibly, righteously and godly was based on the appearing of Jesus.

> For the grace of God has appeared, bringing salvation to all men, instructing us to deny ungodliness and worldly desires and to live sensibly, righteously and godly in the present age, looking for the blessed hope and the appearing of the glory of our great God and Savior, Jesus Christ (Titus 2:11-13).

Peter urged faithfulness and diligence because of the coming day of God.

> Looking for and hastening the coming of the day of God, on account of which the heavens will be destroyed by burning, and the elements will melt with intense heat! But according to His promise we are looking for new heavens and a new earth, in which righteousness dwells. Therefore, beloved, since you look for these things, be diligent to be found by Him in peace, spotless and blameless (2 Peter 3:12-14).

The hope of the future which is tied to the second-coming of Jesus provides an incentive for bold declaration. When Paul discussed the contrast between a ministry that fades and one that has more glory, he spoke of the place of hope.

> Having therefore such a hope, we use great boldness in our speech (2 Corinthians 3:12).

The statement, "Silence is golden," is not a Biblical truth.

The context of Mark 8:27-38 clearly indicated that Jesus' brand of discipleship demanded a choice on the part of the disciples. There are three contrasts in this passage which show the need for choice:

1. In the rebuke of Peter, Jesus said he was setting his mind on

man's interests rather than God's interests. As a disciple of Jesus you will have to decide what your priorities will be when you decide to follow Jesus. Deciding to follow Jesus is the *last* decision that you will make since all future decisions are based on the mind and example of Jesus, your leader.

2. You will have to decide whether you will save your life for your own selfish desires or lose your life in the service of Christ. The disciple cannot live in two worlds at the same time any more than he can love two masters at the same time.

> No one can serve two masters; for either he will hate the one and love the other, or he will hold to one and despise the other. You cannot serve God and mammon (Matthew 6:24).

Perhaps you have watched the TV show "Twilight Zone." The program usually leaves the viewer in confusion because of strange conclusions. In this confused state, the viewer can only guess as to the outcome of the drama. Many disciples have tried to live in some type of in-between world or twilight zone. They realize the foolishness of living in Satan's realm, but lack the commitment to live in Jesus' world. They have opted for a creation of an in-between world. This in-between world does not give them a good feeling about either of the other two realms. They find themselves with enough Christianity that they cannot enjoy their sin and enough sin in their lives that they cannot enjoy their Christianity! What a terrible dilemma to be in. To that dilemma, Jesus demands a choice.

3. You must choose whether you want the whole world at the expense of your soul. Gaining the world distracts you from following Christ.

Jesus knew the experience of potential disciples rejecting Him because of the love of riches. A man desired to know the qualifications of those who would inherit eternal life. Jesus responded by telling him to keep the commandments. The man responded joyfully that he had been. However, when he learned that following Jesus demanded selling his property, he decided the price was too high.

It is so easy to try to get Christianity into ten easy rules, post them on our refrigerator and check them off each day. This approach to religion allows you to feel religious because you obey a few rules. In reality you are still worldly-minded. Discipleship demands more than obeying norms. It demands the transformation of your lifestyle. The temptation of the world is powerful.

> *Do not love the world*, nor the things in the world. If

anyone loves the world, the love of the Father is not in him (1 John 2:15).

For Demas, *having loved this present world*, has deserted me and gone to Thessalonica; Crescens has gone to Galatia, Titus to Dalmatia (2 Timothy 4:10).

Instruct those *who are rich in this present world* not to be conceited or to fix their hope on the uncertainty of riches, but on God, who richly supplies us with all things to enjoy (1 Timothy 6:17).

Disciples must realize that this world is not their home. Disciples are resident-aliens. In the world yes, but of the world—never!

The follower of Jesus is not given the luxury of indecision. Indecision of whether or not you will follow is a decision not to. Jesus drives you to a corner where you are to either love or hate, to be for or against, to be a friend or a foe. To treat the opportunity of discipleship with indifference is a rejection of the invitation of Jesus.

Jesus taught that there had to be a death before there could be much fruit.

Truly, truly, I say to you, unless a grain of wheat falls into the earth and dies, it remains by itself alone; but *if it dies, it bears much fruit* (John 12:24).

The challenge of discipleship in Mark 8:34-38 becomes a commentary on this death. To follow Jesus there must be a death to self (8:34), security (8:35-37) and shame (8:38). Dietrich Bonhoeffer declares that when Jesus calls a man to follow Him He calls "him to come and die."[2] Discipleship is costly and demands your eternal allegiance. You have to write your spiritual obituary before the tag of disciple is placed on you. The disciple cannot live successfully in two worlds without diluting the nature of the call to follow what Jesus had in mind for the entire world.

When the disciple realizes that the call to follow demands death, he forms the basis for transforming his life. When Paul pleaded for a transformed life, he did so on the basis that a death had taken place in the life of the disciple.

If *you have died with Christ* to the elementary principles of the world, why, as if you were living in the world, do you submit yourself to decrees, such as 'Do not handle, do

---

[2]Dietrich Bonhoeffer, *Cost of Discipleship.* (New York: MacMillian Publishing Company, Inc., 1979), p. 99.

not taste, do not touch!' (Colossians 2:20-21).

Set your mind on the things above, not on the things that are on earth. For *you have died* and your life is hidden with Christ in God (Colossians 3:2-3).

Because the disciple has died, he is commanded to "put to death, therefore, whatever belongs to your earthly nature. . ." (Colossians 3:5). No one can be in a position to put to death who has not died himself. When the implications of the disciple's death are realized, conforming to the life of Jesus becomes easier. You do not have to tell a dead man to lie down because that is his nature. The struggle of the disciple is deciding whether or not he really wants to die!

Chapter 5

Mark 10:28-30

Peter began to say to him, 'Behold, we have left everything and followed you.' Jesus said, 'Truly I say to you, there is no one who has left house or brothers or sisters or mother or father or children or farms, for My sake and for the gospel's sake, but that he shall receive a hundred times as much now in the present age, houses and brothers and sisters and mothers and children and farms, along with persecutions; and in the age to come, eternal life' (Mark 10:28-30).

It is not unusual for Peter to serve as the spokesman for the twelve. When Jesus asked who people thought He was, Peter answered (Mark 8:29). Peter rejected the idea of a dying Messiah and represented the thoughts of the twelve (Mark 8:32). On the mount of transfiguration, Peter felt compelled to evaluate the situation (Mark 9:5). When the fig tree withered, Peter articulated the feelings of the twelve (Mark 11:21). One would be caused to wonder how the record of Jesus' ministry would have read had it not been for Peter. Jesus often used Peter's responses as occasions to teach a lesson.

In Mark 10:28-30 Peter is making what he thinks is the necessary response. In the context Jesus had to rebuke the disciples because of their attitude toward the children (Mark 10:13-16). Their attitude toward children was further proof to Jesus that the twelve did not fully understand His ministry. With a military overthrow of Roman garrisons in mind, the disciples felt the children would get in their way and spoil the plan. Jesus uses their misunderstanding of the place of children to teach them a lesson about the kingdom.

> But when Jesus saw this, He was indignant and said to them, 'Permit the children to come to Me; do not hinder them; for the kingdom of God belongs to such as these. Truly I say to you, whoever does not receive the kingdom of God like a child shall not enter it at all' (Mark 10:14-15).

Surely among the lessons He wanted them to learn, one was to listen. They needed to learn to listen rather than to react.

With the teaching about the children still ringing in their ears, Jesus taught the place of wealth in the call to discipleship. The call to follow Him was rejected because of an improper emphasis on wealth (Mark 10:22). Jesus used the rejection of His challenge to follow as an opportunity to teach about the danger of riches. The disciples understood Him to say that this type of priority would make it impossible to enter the kingdom. Jesus was not saying wealthy people could not enter the kingdom, but the object of their allegiance was to follow Jesus. Jesus challenged the would-be disciple to count the cost of what he believed to be important.

Peter was viewing this whole discourse and felt he had to say something. Peter was quick to point out that the twelve had responded in the same way that Jesus desired of the man who inquired about eternal life. Jesus saw quickly the need to point out to Peter a broader scope than he had seen.

1. Followed Jesus

If there was anything the disciples had straight, it was the focal point of their following. They were in a small fog as to the definition of following, but not as to whom to follow. The disciples never took their eyes off Jesus even though their minds were somewhere else.

We might criticize Peter for a lot of misunderstandings, but he didn't misunderstand who to follow. It was this type of determination that led Peter to follow Jesus when it would have been easier to fall by the wayside. When the council asked Peter and John "not to speak or teach at all in the name of Jesus," they gave a classic response.

> . . . Whether it is right in the sight of God to give heed to you rather than to God, you be the judge; for we cannot stop speaking what *we have seen and heard* (Acts 4:19-20).

It was this type of determination that made Peter remain loyal when threatened. Peter's unwavering determination to follow in spite of the number of times he stumbled is an example for us today. Keeping your eyes on Jesus will lead to some valleys and peaks, but will finally lead you to the Father.

2. Experienced Persecutions

In this passage Jesus did not mention that He desired His followers to be fishers of men as He did in Mark 1:17-18. He was doing something similar to what He did in the Mark 8:34-38 passage by giving further depth to what it meant to be a fisher of men. Not only did every Galilean fisherman know that it would take self-denial to catch fish, but there would be opposition (persecution) in order to be a successful fisherman. The experienced Galilean fisherman knew full well that successful fishing demanded both knowing the habits of fish and being willing to compete with the obstacles. The elements were not always helpful. Sometimes the best fishing took place at inconvenient hours. The fisherman had to practice continued perseverance, realizing the next throw of the net could mean the catch of the day.

As Jesus helped His disciples to better understand the depths of following, He knew that they would have to understand that their assault on the world to catch men would meet with some opposition. Had Jesus explained the difficulties in Mark 1:17-18, the disciples would not have been mature enough to handle it. Later in Mark, Jesus became even more specific as to the nature of the opposition. Jesus said the opposition would come in many forms. It might come from his home (Matthew 10:36). The disciples would be delivered to the courts, beaten in the synagogue, or they would stand before governors and kings (Mark 13:9).

Jesus was a living example of the lifestyle to which He was calling them. They watched the opposition during His lifetime, and they saw even more before He finally went to the cross. The church in Acts is an example of a literal fulfillment of the prediction of Jesus in reference to persecution. This invasion of the kingdom of Satan is not going to meet with approval by the forces of evil. Persecution is inevitable if the disciples of Jesus make continuous frontal attacks against the forces of evil. The preparation of Jesus' teachings on discipleship provide the backdrop for future teachings.

And indeed, all who desire to live godly in Christ Jesus *will be persecuted* (2 Timothy 3:12).

3. Left Everything

Peter echoed in 10:28 what had taken place earlier in the lives of the disciples in 1:17-20. If the disciples understood any part of discipleship, it was that it was going to be costly. However, it needs to be observed that the disciples with their concept of some type of military overthrow of Rome still lingering in their minds, could have thought of sacrifice in a militant vein rather than one of spiritual warfare.

Peter wanted to make sure that Jesus did not think the twelve had made the same mistake as the man who inquired about eternal life. If leaving everything is a mark of true discipleship, Peter was making sure Jesus knew what they had done. Actually it was not necessary to remind Jesus of their great sacrifice because Jesus knew what had taken place in their lives. The twelve might have left many physical things, but they were not ashamed about asking for places of importance (Mark 10:35-37). James and John's request (they were not the only ones seeking power positions, Mark 9:34) shows their unwillingness to give up self and be the servant Jesus called them to be.

There was not anything that the disciples had left that Jesus could not match in His personal sacrifice. As Jesus had called upon them to be willing to leave family for Him, the disciples had seen this fulfilled in His life during their ministry with Him. In an attempt to escape the press of the ministry to people, Jesus went home. Instead of home being a place of rest and relaxation, it was just the opposite.

> And He came home and the multitude gathered again, to such an extent that they could not even eat a meal. And when His own people heard of this, they went out to take custody of Him; for they were saying, 'He has lost His senses' (Mark 3:20-21).

After Jesus had taught concerning the divided kingdom in answer to the false accusation that He was possessed by Beelzebub (Mark 3:22-30), His mother and brothers came to Him. When He was told of their arrival, He placed a new definition on mother and brothers.

> And answering them, He said, 'Who are My mother and My brothers?' And looking about on those who were sitting around Him, He said, 'Behold, My mother and My brothers! For whoever does the will of God, he is My brother and sister and mother' (Mark 3:33-35).

Jesus was not asking His disciples to give up something that He had not given up.

It is impossible for someone to "out sacrifice" Jesus. He stands as a model for the present disciple to imitate. As you look at Jesus, growing in sacrifice is always needful.

4. Receive Hundred-fold Now and Eternal Life

God didn't call upon man to give up anything that He didn't repay in greater measure. However, this was the first time that Jesus promised a hundred-fold return on the investment that the disciple had made in following Jesus. What greater motivation could Jesus have given the disciples than a return of a hundred times their investment, plus the promise of eternal life! Every company recognizes the importance of incentives to motivate salesmen to work hard. There is no earthly company that begins to match the incentives for hard work that Jesus has given.

A legitimate question can be raised as to why these incentives were placed in this context. The sacrifice of family (mother, father, brothers and sisters) and the threat of persecution are offset by the hundred-fold return and eternal life. The principle of "the pain is worth the gain" is demonstrated by Jesus' reward incentives. The losses of the disciples were more than offset by the gains of hundred-fold return and eternal life. "All this and heaven too" represents a great bargain for the disciple of Jesus.

It is interesting to note that Jesus mentioned leaving one's father in 10:29, but when He talked about the return in 10:30, father was not mentioned. This ommission could have been quite intentional because the disciples had a Father who was in heaven (Mark 11:25). The father one gained in his response to follow Jesus was far greater than the one he gave up.

The fulfillment of the promises of Jesus was demonstrated in the lives of the early disciples again and again. The disciples found a family everywhere they went. They felt and experienced a closeness with brethren of different countries and different races. What is exciting about Jesus' promise of hundred-fold return is that it can be claimed by the disciples of Jesus today. Have you ever gone to a strange city and found other brethren who were following Jesus? Wasn't it exciting to see them open up their homes to "strangers" and share a meal with you? The true disciple of Jesus has family and friends around the world! Some of your spiritual family are closer and dearer to you than some of your blood relatives. We can all rejoice that the promise of Christ is for the disciple today who will say that he is willing to leave everything and follow Jesus!

41

Chapter 6

Luke 9:57-62

And as they were going along the road, someone said to Him, 'I will follow You wherever You go.' And Jesus said to him, 'The foxes have holes, and the birds of the air have nests, but the Son of Man has nowhere to lay His head.' And He said to another, 'Follow Me.' But he said, 'Permit me first to go and bury my father.' But He said to him, 'Allow the dead to bury their own dead; but as for you, go and proclaim everywhere the kingdom of God.' And another also said, 'I will follow You, Lord; but first permit me to say good-bye to those at home.' But Jesus said to him, 'No one, after putting his hand to the plow and looking back, is fit for the kingdom of God' (Luke 9:57-62).

Jesus was determined to go to Jerusalem (Luke 9:51-52). Luke makes it very clear concerning Jesus' determination to get to Jerusalem (13:22; 17:11; 18:31; 19:11, 28 and 41). Jesus realized He had a meeting with destiny in the city. On His journey to Jerusalem, He took several occasions to stop and challenge people to follow Him. After Jesus had rebuked the disciples for wanting to burn the Samaritan village for not receiving Him, He announced again His mission in which He wanted them to share: not to destroy men's lives but to save them (9:56).

At some point on the road to Jerusalem, He encountered three responses to His challenge of discipleship. The first response was from the impetuous disciple. He gave a response to Jesus even though the record did not show that Jesus asked for one. He volunteered himself to the service of Christ without really giving it much thought. He became an example of the type of soil Jesus spoke of in the parable of the sower.

And those on the rocky soil are those who, when they hear, receive the word with joy; and these have no firm root; they believe for a while, and in time of temptation fall away (Luke 8:13).

Jesus was not about to enlist him in His army without telling him something about cost counting. Having a place to live is important to most people. Jesus thought He would quickly put the potential disciple to the test by explaining His lifestyle, which in turn would be the disciple's lifestyle. When Jesus explained that the foxes and the birds had more physical security than He had, I am sure it put a whole new light on this person's following.

When you decide to follow Jesus, you should not be swept away with the excitement of the moment and the prospect for adventure, but should realize what will be demanded of you. Even when this is done, a better understanding will come with time.

Deciding to follow Jesus is similar to the decision to get married. It should not be made hastily or without some consideration of what is involved in the decision. However, in spite of all the preparation you make for marriage, many things are learned after you get married that you don't expect. It is at this point in a marriage that the commitment to make it work out becomes the tie that keeps the couple together.

You will learn things after you become a disciple that were not very clear to you when you said, "I will follow Jesus," but that solid commitment to stick with the Master will allow you the ability to weather all of the adjustments.

The second response to the challenge to follow finds a procrastinating follower. He wanted to go home and bury his father. There is a good possibility that the father at home was not dead yet. The reason for believing this is that if the father were dead, the man would not have been with Jesus in the first place, but would have been at home attending to the affairs of the funeral. In Jewish thought, burial was of utmost importance and demanded one's full attention. The responsibility of burial would be considered more important than the killing of the Passover sacrifice, the performance of circumcision, or the study of the Law. Assuming that this was the case, that his father was still alive, Jesus could not wait for him to go home and wait for his father's death. This could have meant a delay of an indefinite period. Jesus responded by telling him that the dead (the ones without spiritual insight or concerns) take care of the dead. He was calling them to a greater and more demanding service. They needed to go and proclaim the kingdom of God everywhere.

The third response came from a family-oriented man. It appears he had been listening to these conversations. He explained that he desired to follow, but he needed to go home for one more visit. On the surface this does not sound like an unreasonable request to make, but the Master Teacher detected a little reluctance on the part of this potential follower. It was at this point that Jesus said that the challenge to follow Him had to be answered by those who were not wanting to look back, but would continue to work with their eyes straight ahead.

Woven through these three responses to Jesus are similar demands to discipleship as have been seen in the three passages in Mark. The narration in Luke is different from Mark, but the expectations of Jesus for His followers remain the same.

1. Follow Me

It is quite clear concerning the object of the following—Jesus. Jesus gives the demand and according to the material in the text, two of them respond in a similar way without being asked. The call to follow is clear: to duplicate in the disciple's life, the life of the one who calls.

2. Go and Proclaim the Kingdom Everywhere

In this statement Jesus shows the importance of telling the good news to all the world. This is another case where Jesus is calling the disciples to a work in which He is already engaged.

> And Jesus was going about in all Galilee, teaching in their synagogues, and *proclaiming the gospel of the kingdom*, and healing every kind of disease and every kind of sickness among the people (Matthew 4:23).

Jesus' work and proclamation became known in all Syria, from Jerusalem to the Decapolis and beyond the Jordan (Matthew 4:24-25). Uppermost in the mind of Jesus was getting the message of the good news to all the world. The parting words of Jesus prior to His ascension show the same urgency.

> And He said to them, '*Go into all the world* and preach the gospel to all creation' (Mark 16:15).

> *Go therefore and make disciples of all the nations*, baptizing them in the name of the Father and the Son and the Holy Spirit (Matthew 28:19).

3. No Home

Most of us know the emotional pull of home. We have all taken long trips to get home. As we near this important place in our lives, our cars seem to want to go faster. Even though Jesus had plenty of places to stay, He did not have that security of the one place He could go if all else failed. Jesus warned the inquirers that the same could be expected of them if they chose to follow Him. God always provides for our needs, but we must be willing to give up that which has much meaning for us if necessary. It is very clear that a price is to be paid.

When confronted with the decision to follow Jesus, it is very easy to make excuses why we can't. Instead of making excuses, we need to make commitments. We can go through our whole lives trying to explain why we did not do something, when the truth of the matter is that we lack courage to make a definite and final decision.

4. Keep Plowing

It is not the intention of Jesus for anyone to begin to follow Him and then fall by the wayside. Jesus wants the type of faithfulness He had to His Father to be characteristic of His followers. One of the best ways to stay faithful is to keep plowing and looking ahead. If one ever stops to look back, he will either go back, quit plowing, not plow a straight line or possibly run into something.

The implementation of this important principle is seen clearly in the admonition of Paul to the young preacher.

> Pay close attention to yourself and to your teaching; persevere in these things; for as you do this you will insure salvation both for yourself and for those who hear you (1 Timothy 4:16).

When you stay active in saving others, you ensure your own salvation. Some of the greatest spiritual highs in your life are when you are actively working in someone else's life. To a large degree, your faithfulness in discipleship can be traced back to your continuous efforts to proclaim the kingdom.

Besides the example of Jesus and the demands of His discipleship, there is another good reason for the disciple to be working in the lives of others. The disciple's own self-preservation is at stake. Paul encouraged Timothy to continue because he saved others as well as himself (1 Timothy 4:16). The disciple cannot expect to survive spiritually with simply a good defense against the darts of Satan. No athletic team with only a defense will be a winner no matter how good it might be. If a team doesn't score on offense nor develop a plan to score, the opposition, even though weak, will some way score a point.

Chapter 7
Luke 14:25-33

Now great multitudes were going along with Him; and He turned and said to them, 'If anyone comes to Me, and does not hate his own father and mother and wife and children and brothers and sister, yes, and even his own life, he cannot be My disciple. Whoever does not carry his own cross and come after Me cannot be My disciple. For which one of you, when he wants to build a tower, does not first sit down and calculate the cost, to see if he has enough to complete it? Otherwise, when he has laid a foundation, and is not able to finish, all who observe it begin to ridicule him, saying, "This man began to build and was not able to finish." Or what king, when he sets out to meet another king in battle, will not first sit down and take counsel whether he is strong enough with ten thousand men to encounter the one coming against him with twenty thousand? Or else, while the other is still far away, he sends a delegation and asks terms of peace. So therefore, no one of you can be My disciple who does not give up all his own possessions.

Where ever Jesus traveled, He attracted crowds. Some of these people came to see the miracles. Because of His spreading fame, some came out of curiosity. However, there was an element that was very sincere and wanted to know if He were really the Messiah. They really wanted to know what it meant to follow Him.

There is probably not a more challenging passage in the entire New Testament on discipleship than this one. Jesus has never been this pointed in His other challenges. It would appear from a human point of view that Jesus would drive everyone away with these types of strong demands, but He didn't. The stronger the challenge, the greater the response.

Several years ago when the Peace Corp concept was formed, many thought that the "soft youth" of America would not respond, but how wrong they were! What would happen in America if the true demands of discipleship would begin ringing loud and clear? I am sure that several who would want to stay worldly and religious at the same time would leave, but you would be left with a community of believers who would be a living testimony to the truth of the gospel.

In this passage we will find the basic ingredients of discipleship that we have found in the preceding passages. Jesus might put them in a different form and express them in different language, but the concepts of what it really means to follow are always there. Jesus knew what kind of following it was going to take to reach the world with the good news, and He was not about to compromise His demands.

1. Must Come to Jesus

Jesus introduces this demand by making Himself the focal point of the coming. To accent what it means to come to Him, He contrasts the love that the disciple must have for him in comparison to the love he has for others. This comparison is stressed by the use of the word "hate." First, Jesus uses this to show what should have first loyalty in the life of the disciple. There is no place in the ministry of Jesus for literal hate of another individual even if he is an enemy (Luke 6:27). To love someone else more than another individual is sometimes spoken of as "hate." Joseph loved Rachel more than he did Leah; however, the next verse tells that the Lord saw that Leah was "hated" (Genesis 29:30-31, RSV). (See Deuteronomy 12:15 for another example of the use of this word.) Second, Jesus uses the word "hate" to show the comparison of the love the disciple is to have for him in contrast to the love he is to have for others. So great is the allegiance of the disciple to Jesus that every other relationship could be classified as "hate" or "love-less."

2. Must Carry His Own Cross

The meaning and implications of the cross were discussed when the Mark 8:34-38 passage was considered. However, there is something added in Luke that is not in Mark which makes cross-bearing even more personal. In Mark, Jesus commands the disciple to bear "his cross" which simply means everyone has a responsibility which is their own. In Luke, Jesus commands the disciple to bear "his own cross." This means not only does everyone have his own cross, but the emphasis is upon the disciple *himself* doing the bearing. It is something that he alone can do. The disciple is called upon to do what in a short period of time Jesus will do (John 19:17).

In Luke 9:23-26, you will find the parallel account to Mark 8:34-38. There is one major addition to the challenge in Luke that is not found in Mark. In Luke Jesus challenges His disciples to take up their crosses *daily*. The responsibility of cross-bearing cannot be taken up and laid down at will, but is to be an activity of the disciple of Jesus. He is to be involved daily, telling others about the love and concern of God for them. It is with this type of foundation that we find the early disciples in Acts being consistent in their daily bearing the cross of Jesus.

> And *day by day* continuing with one mind in the temple, and breaking bread from house to house, they were taking their meals together with gladness and sincerity of heart, praising God, and having favor with all the people. And the Lord was adding to their number day by day those who were being saved (Acts 2:46-47).

> And *every day*, in the temple and from house to house, they kept right on teaching and preaching Jesus as the Christ (Acts 5:42).

> And the churches were being strengthened in the faith, and were increasing in number *daily* (Acts 16:5).

> So he was reasoning in the synagogue with the Jews and the God-fearing Gentiles, and in the market place *every day* with those who happened to be present (Acts 17:17).

> But when some were becoming hardened and disobedient, speaking evil of the Way before the multitude, he withdrew from them and took away the disciples, reasoning *daily* in the school of Tyrannus (Acts 19:9).

Involved in accepting the cross is accepting the will of God for the life of the disciple. When the disciple accepts the will of God for his life, he accepts the will of God for the lives of all men. The will of God for all men is that they might be saved.

> Who desires *all men to be saved* and to come to the knowledge of the truth (1 Timothy 2:4).

> The Lord is not slow about His promise, as some count slowness, but is patient toward you, *not wishing for any to perish* but for all to come to repentance (2 Peter 3:9).

> For this is the will of My Father, that *everyone* who beholds the Son and believes in Him, *may have eternal life;* and I Myself will raise him up on the last day (John 6:40).

It is unheard of for the disciple to claim to be bearing his own cross and not be involved in that for which the Savior died. How can being a fisher of men be optional to the disciple when the salvation of the world is heart and core of a loving Father? No disciple who takes seriously his cross-bearing can take lightly the need to share the message of salvation with a lost world. The problem of getting the message to the world is not methods, but men. As the religious world looks for better methods to get the message out, God is looking for better men. When disciples become committed to cross-bearing, methods of dispersing the message will be found. What greater way to send a message than through a person redeemed by the blood of Christ? When God wanted to tell the world of His love, He wrapped the message up in a person (John 3:16).

3. Cannot Be Possessed by Others, Self or Things

In the challenge to discipleship, Jesus compares loyalties that disciples would have to other objects with the loyalty he must have to the Savior. Jesus is not teaching disrespect for one's family. No teacher ever gave more sanctity and respect for the home than Jesus. If the teachings of Jesus were followed in reference to how family members should be treated, what a beautiful world this would be (see 1 Timothy 5:8). However, in Luke, Jesus is saying that the loyalty to them cannot be the same as loyalty to Him. You cannot be possessed by them and in the same manner be possessed by Jesus.

The underlying theme of Luke 14:26-27 is that the disciple cannot even be possessed by himself. Self is at the heart of all sin. You cannot be overly involved in a love for self without running into conflict with loyalties. The idolatry of self-centeredness is a hard one to tear down in the life of the disciple.

To qualify for discipleship, you cannot be possessed by the "things" the world has to offer. Materialism has always been a barrier to discipleship. Putting our possessions before following Jesus is attacked by Him. How many have lost their zeal for God because of a second job? How many times have the luxuries of life become the necessities? Trying to abide by the philosophy of "keeping up with the Joneses" has led many families into problems that hindered their discipleship. (If your philosophy is to try to keep up with the Joneses, watch out! They will refinance!!)

In Luke 14:25-33, Jesus said three times that unless a certain thing is true, you "cannot be my disciple" (14:26, 27, and 33). Each time, it is in the context of being possessed by others (14:26), self (14:26b-27) and things (14:33). If you are serious about discipleship, it is obvious that there is a price to be paid. Jesus never does

49

apologize about the high cost of discipleship. Since both the Father and Son paid a high price, there can be no end of the year sales for Their followers.

The cost of following Jesus is further taught by the use of twin parables (a man building a tower and the king going to war). Jesus wants to make sure His disciples know what is in store for them. When any decision in life is made, the pluses and minuses must be considered. Entering into any major decision of life strictly on the emotion of the hour is not necessarily the best way. The twin parables show the importance of counting the cost. In one case if you fail to do so, you can become the laughing stock of the community. In the second case, you can experience defeat with all the humility that comes with it.

4. Finish the Task

The twin parables show the importance of finishing what you begin. No one wants to start something and not finish it. In the same manner, Jesus doesn't want people to begin to follow Him and not complete the course.

There are some slight differences in the parables. In the builder parable, the man, by his own will, chose to build. In the war parable, the king did not have a choice of whether or not he wanted to fight, but was just invaded by another king. The king's choice is that he must react to a situation that is not of his own choosing. The lessons of both parables are close, but slightly different. In the first parable, the disciple is depicted as sitting down and deciding if he can really afford to follow Jesus. In the second parable, the disciple has to decide whether or not he can afford to refuse the demands of Jesus. Completion of the building project and the victory at battle are both the desired goals of the two parables. Crossing the finish line is the goal of every disciple. In the two parables Jesus is not trying to discourage the disciple, but is trying to get him to decide at the beginning whether or not he will finish the task.

We have all witnessed people who have failed at tasks they started. There might be many reasons why someone fails to complete a task, but most of the time it can be attributed to a lack of determination. Dogged determination will overcome many obstacles on the road to victory. Once, two men were discussing their adventures in the jungles. One man told of being chased by a lion. When he was almost ready to collapse, he saw a limb fifteen feet above the trail and leaped for it. His anxious friend said, "Did you reach it?" His friend replied, "No, but I caught it on the way down!" That is determination! It is that type of determination that will cause you to finish the task of following Jesus regardless of the obstacles in your way.

Chapter 8

The Gospel of John

The study of the passages in Mark and Luke (there are some parallel accounts in Matthew) have shown us the demand of discipleship. The gospel of John was written many years later than Matthew, Mark and Luke. John was written about 95 AD, which would put it approximately thirty-five years after the writing of the other accounts of the life of Jesus. The gospel of John does not contain the concise passages on discipleship that were found in the other accounts, but the book has a great deal to say about discipleship. The purpose of the book was to get people to believe (John 20:31). Realizing that the books of the New Testament were written to be read at one sitting, you will easily be able to see that the basic demands of discipleship found in the other accounts are seen clearly in John.

1. Abide in His Word

> Jesus therefore was saying to those Jews who had believed Him, 'If you abide in My word, then you are truly *disciples of Mine*' (John 8:31).

Jesus defined His disciples as ones who abide in His word. Jesus, who is the Word (John 1:1-4), is connected with the word or sayings He had spoken.

> There is a judge for the one who rejects me and does not accept my words; that very word which I spoke will condemn him at the last day (John 12:48, NIV).

You cannot be a follower of Jesus without abiding in His word. The word instructs the disciple about how he is to live. The word points you to the Messiah whom you must follow. Paul declared to the Colossians: "Let the word of Christ richly dwell within you" (Colossians 3:16). When you are consumed by the word of Christ, you will be a follower of Christ.

The disciple studies the scriptures for the purpose of learning the mind of Christ. To read the word to confirm what you already

51

believe is not reading the word with an open and receptive mind. The word of God is not meant to be a "debater's handbook," but a revelation of the mind of Christ to His followers. James gives a very practical way to view the word.

> Therefore putting aside all filthiness and all that remains of wickedness, in humility to receive the word implanted, which is able to save your souls. But *prove yourselves doers of the word*, and not merely hearers who delude themselves (James 1:21-22).

Jesus connects Himself with the word His Father has spoken. A rejection of Jesus is tantamount to the rejection of the Father's word.

> And the Father who sent Me, He has borne witness of Me. You have neither heard His voice at any time, nor seen His form. And you do not have His word abiding in you, for you do not believe Him whom He sent. You search the Scriptures, because you think that in them you have eternal life; and it is these that bear witness of Me; and you are unwilling to come to Me, that you may have life (John 5:37-40).

Jesus said they searched the scriptures, but they still did not accept Him. If we are not open to the truths of the scriptures, we will not see the Savior we claim to follow. Wouldn't it be great if the whole world had the attitude of the people in the city of Berea!

> And the brethren immediately sent Paul and Silas away by night to Berea; and when they arrived, they went into the synagogue of the Jews. Now these were more noble-minded than those in Thessalonica, for *they received the word with great eagerness, examining the Scriptures daily*, to see whether these things were so (Acts 17:10-11).

2. Bear Fruit

> By this is My Father glorified, that *you bear much fruit*, and so prove to be My disciples (John 15:8).

Jesus said that His Father is glorified when His disciples bear much fruit. Not only does Jesus expect His disciples to bear much fruit, but the fruit must remain (John 15:16). The disciples will produce after their own kind, more disciples. Not only will disciples want to show in their lives the fruits of the Spirit (Galatians 5:19-21), but they will also have a desire to produce others like

52

themselves, i.e. followers of the Christ and partakers of the true vine which is Christ.

> *I am the vine*, you are the branches; he who abides in Me, and I in him, he bears much fruit; for apart from Me you can do nothing (John 15:5).

Paul said that his purpose for going to Rome was to have some fruit among the Gentiles.

> And I do not want you to be unaware, brethren, that often I have planned to come to you (and have been prevented thus far) in order that *I might obtain some fruit among you* also, even as among the rest of the Gentiles (Romans 1:13).

As the fisherman was trained to catch fish, the disciple who abides in the vine is to bear much fruit of like kind. It is inconceivable that a disciple blessed by following the Christ would not want the same blessing for others. When you find something good for your life, it does not take a command or rule to get you to share it with others. The disciple who abides in Christ will produce the fruit that Christ desires for his life. It is the desire of Christ that all men abide in Him, and thereby the salvation of the world still be accomplished. The disciple who bears fruit is fulfilling in this life the purpose that Christ had for all the world. Jesus wanted the white fields that were ready for harvest (John 4:35) to be gathered by His disciples. As a fisher of men and as a fruit-bearer, the disciple is fulfilling God's eternal purpose for the world: that all mankind become the family of God.

3. Love One Another

> A new commandment I give to you, that *you love one another*, even as I have loved you, that you also love one another. By this all men will know that you are My disciples, if you have love for one another (John 13:34-35).

Following Jesus is not without effort and sacrifice on the part of the disciple. It would first appear that loving one another would not be difficult in order to prove to be a disciple of Jesus, but it is impossible to truly love without sacrifice. The sacrificial love of the disciple is directed to two different objects:

1. The disciple must love the world as Jesus did. When we do not

love men for God, we invalidate God's message of love for men. Jesus loved the world in spite of what it was and what it did to Him, and because of what it could potentially be. Sacrificial love demands the acceptance of the rejection and scorns of the world. Jesus told His disciples not to be alarmed if the world hated them since it also hated Him (John 15:18). The cost for the disciple to love the world is not cheap.

2. The disciple must love his fellow disciples. Jesus declared that He was going away and that the disciples could not follow (John 13:33). During His earthly ministry the world knew who the disciple of Jesus was as they saw him in His presence. However, when He left, how did the world determine who the followers of Jesus were? The way they loved one another was going to be the way the world would know.

Jesus said the mark which will distinguish His disciple is "loving one another as I have loved you." Loving one another is not a new commandment, but the newness is found in the phrase, "as I have loved you." Jesus loved His disciples in spite of their shallowness, misunderstanding and desire for preeminence. If the disciple has the same love for his fellow disciples that Jesus had for His disciples a certain sacrifice is necessary. Jesus did not say that the world would know His disciples by their advertisements, debates or religious papers, but by their love. As the poet has put it:

> To live with saints in heaven
> Is all bliss and glory.
> To live with saints on earth
> Is quite another story.

The disciple cannot love his fellow disciples without giving time and effort. Working with one another through the victories and the defeats of life is costly. The disciple runs the risk of being rejected and misunderstood by the very one he seeks to influence. This is the risk that love must run. Jesus was rejected and misunderstood, and even betrayed, by the very ones He spent time with and loved deeply.

4. Walk Faithfully With Him

As a result of this many of His disciples withdrew, and were not walking with Him any more. Jesus said therefore to the twelve, 'You do not want to go away also, do you?' Simon Peter answered Him, 'Lord, to whom shall we go? You have the words of eternal life' (John

6:66-68).

The *true* disciples are those who continue to follow in spite of Jesus' difficult statement (John 6:60). The faithfulness demanded in discipleship is shown in Peter's determination to follow in spite of the actions of those who withdrew. Discipleship is not only responding to the challenge of Jesus, but it is continuing to respond in face of opposition and the challenging teaching of Jesus. To begin a journey is not as difficult as finishing the journey. Many begin that journey, but when the obstacles become great, the tendency to drop out is there.

> Nevertheless many even of the rulers believed in Him, but because of the Pharisees they were not confessing Him, lest they should be put out of the synagogue; for *they loved the approval of men rather than the approval of God* (John 12:42-43).

Discipleship does not allow anyone to go AWOL (absent without leave) nor to retire from active duty. The retirement benefits of the disciple are "out of this world." Faithfulness and fidelity are important for true discipleship. The only time the disciple can quit following is when he is transferred from the "field" to the "home office." This transfer has to be considered a promotion. The death of the disciple has to be considered his graduation to glory and should be consummated with a victory celebration.

> Precious in the sight of the Lord is the death of his saints (Psalm 116:15, NIV).

Conclusion

The demand of discipleship as revealed in the gospels showed some strong correlations. They are not exactly parallel in every way, but the ingredients of the demand are basically found in all the passages considered. As God planned beforehand—before the foundation of the world (Revelation 13:8)—that His Son would be slain, He determined the type of following He desired for the crowning acts of His creation made in His image (Genesis 1:26). The antiquity of the demand of discipleship is seen in the lives of two Old Testament men. The same four elements of discipleship that have been clearly shown from gospel accounts can be traced through the lives of these men. The first example of an Old Testament disciple is Moses.

1. Believed in the "I Am"

Moses had been reared to believe in God. The burning bush incident confirmed his belief in God. When God spoke to him, he quickly answered "Here am I" (Exodus 3:4). In spite of the difficulties and the excuses of Moses, he did have a great belief in God. When Moses realized the task before him, he raised a question for God.

> Behold, I am going to the sons of Israel, and I shall say to them, 'The God of your fathers has sent me to you.' Now they may say to me, 'What is His name?' What shall I say to them? And God said to Moses, 'I AM WHO I AM;' and He said, 'Thus you shall say to the sons of Israel, I AM has sent me to you' (Exodus 3:13-14).

Only a man who had a strong faith in God would have confronted the leader of the greatest nation at that time. Moses had a committed allegiance to the great I Am.

2. Preached the Message of God

Moses repeated the message of God in the presence of Pharaoh on more than one occasion. He was not afraid of the monarch of Egypt because he represented a God greater than all the Egyptian gods put together. Moses was not afraid to speak to the people of Israel when they needed a strong rebuke. He preached a message of commitment to God.

> *Dedicate yourselves today to the Lord*—for every man has been against his son and against his brother—in order that He may bestow a blessing upon you today' (Exodus 32:29).

Even though he was a man who claimed to be slow of speech, he thundered out the message of God on many occasions.

3. Paid a Price to Follow God

Moses was in line to become the leader of the powerful country of Egypt. However, he chose following his God over the offsprings of the Egyptian courts. The best description of this price is found in God's Hall of Fame—Hebrews 11.

> By faith Moses, when he had grown up, refused to be called the son of Pharaoh's daughter; choosing rather to endure ill-treatment with the people of God, than to en-

joy the passing pleasures of sin; considering the reproach of Christ greater than the treasures of Egypt; for he was looking to the reward. By faith he left Egypt, not fearing the wrath of the king; for he endured, as seeing Him who is unseen (Hebrews 11:24-27).

To exchange a shepherd's staff, the herding of the sheep of Jethro, and the leadership of the fickle people of Israel for the throne of an Egyptian Pharaoh was quite a price to pay.

4. Faithful to the End

Even though Moses was dedicated to God, his life was not free from mistakes. I am sure he would have liked to relive some parts so he could do them differently. However, in spite of some "strike outs" in his life, he was still allowed to go "home." He is grouped with the redeemed of the ages (Matthew 17:3). Isn't it great that our batting averages for God do not appear on a daily basis? God knows our daily activities, but it's our over-all life and "average" that really counts.

Noah is the second example of the antiquity of the demand of discipleship.

1. Believed in God

Noah was a man who was committed to following God even though his fellow man was not.

But Noah found favor in the eyes of the Lord. These are the records of the generations of Noah. Noah was a righteous man, blameless in his time; Noah walked with God (Genesis 6:8-9).

2. Preached

He was a preacher of righteousness (2 Peter 2:5). Surely the world needed one who was willing to reach out to it because of its sinfulness (Genesis 6:5).

3. Sacrificed

Noah paid the price of the insults of the world because of his willingness to build a boat on dry ground, getting ready for something that had never happened before. It must have been a lonely life while the ark was being built.

57

4. Faithful to the Task

Noah's faithfulness is seen in building the ark according to God's plan and in his faithfulness during the many years of construction. When many would have quit, he kept going.

The correlation in the demands of discipleship indicate God had a plan of response for His creation. The following chart indicates the correlations of the demand of discipleship:

1. Object of Discipleship
   a. Follow Me (Mark 1:17)
   b. Must desire to follow Jesus (Mark 8:34)
   c. Followed Jesus (Mark 10:28)
   d. Follow Me (Luke 9:59,61)
   e. Must come to Jesus (Luke 14:26)
   f. Abide in His word (John 8:31)
2. Purpose of Discipleship
   a. Become fishers of men (Mark 1:17)
   b. Must deny self and take up his cross (Mark 8:34)
   c. Experienced persecutions (Mark 10:30)
   d. Go and proclaim everywhere the Kingdom (Luke 9:60)
   e. Must carry his own cross (Luke 14:27)
   f. Bear fruit (John 15:8)
3. Cost of Discipleship
   a. Leave occupation (Mark 1:18)
   b. Lose life to find it (Mark 8:35)
   c. Left everything (Mark 10:28)
   d. No home (Luke 9:58)
   e. Cannot be possessed by others, self or things (Luke 14:26-27,33)
   f. Love one another (John 8:35)
4. Results of Discipleship
   a. Followed Jesus (Mark 1:18,20)
   b. Must not be ashamed of Jesus (Mark 8:38)
   c. Receive hundred-fold now and eternal life (Mark 10:30)
   d. Keep plowing (Luke 9:62)
   e. Finish the task (Luke 14:28-32)
   f. Walk faithfully with Him (John 6:66-69)

It is inconceivable that God would have a purpose for the world and leave man to his own devices as to how to respond to that plan. The pattern of response to the call to discipleship by Jesus is further demonstrated in the events that followed the ascension. The events

58

that followed the life and teachings of Jesus demonstrate the purpose that God has for His followers.

The growth of the following of Jesus as revealed in Acts and various epistles is helpful to show the first century expression of what following Jesus was like. Every disciple must realize that he must begin with the demand of Jesus as revealed in the gospels before he can demonstrate that demand in his life in a practical way. The power to be what God wants us to be is not in duplicating the demonstration in the first century, but in tapping into the power that made the demonstration in the first century. The power to become what God intended for us to be can be traced to our personal response to the man from Nazareth. It is by our commitment to His lifestyle that we can become "recreated" into the image of our creator.

Section III

Demonstration of Discipleship

The design for discipleship has been established by examining the nature of God and His revelation in Jesus Christ. The demand was formed from the design and became an extension of God. The pattern of the demand was established by looking at key discipleship passages in the gospels. The same four-part pattern of the demand (which was an extension of the design of discipleship as manifested in Jesus and rooted in God) will be seen in the demonstration of discipleship in the church in Acts, the Thessalonian church and in the lives of Paul and Barnabas.

The demonstration of discipleship is a natural outgrowth of the design and demand. Since Jesus is the reflection of His Father and His demands are an extension of what He is, it stands to reason that the first century church continued to manifest this pattern. The nature of the church is rooted in the person of Jesus. The church was involved in a faithful proclamation, compassionate service and a loving fellowship because this is the way the early disciples viewed Jesus. A Jesus-centered church is not possible in any century unless one returns to an emphasis on Jesus. It is a mistake to try to reproduce the church in the first century without the reality that produced that church—Jesus. The church is a reflection of a greater reality. When only the reflection is produced, the substance of the reality is lost. This does not mean that the church in the first century serves no purpose for us today. It shows how the demands of discipleship were demonstrated in a practical way. The power and success of the first century church is not solely found in its organization, but in the basis and background which is found in the demand of Jesus.

The outgrowth of the ministry of Jesus as seen in the early church and individual disciples becomes further proof of God's eternal purpose for His creation. The pattern for following what God desired for all became increasingly clear to me as the early church came under close examination with the nature of God, the personality of Jesus and the demands of Jesus' teaching forming the basis for the study.

Chapter 9

The Church in Acts

The church in Acts is a picture or reflection of the discipleship concept as taught by Jesus, recorded in the gospels. The church in Acts is an outgrowth of the seeds planted by Jesus as He taught what it meant to follow. The church in Acts was the "effect" and Jesus' teaching on discipleship was the "cause" of the effect. The difference between the demand in the gospels and the demonstration in Acts is in extent of coverage. The church in Acts shows the pattern of discipleship in the eternal purpose of God.

1. Stressed Christ

The study of the sermons in Acts leaves little doubt concerning the important place of Jesus in the lives of the early disciples. As the sun is to the solar system, so is Christ to Christianity.

Peter's first sermon in Acts 2, which opened the door of the church to the Jewish nation, centered in Jesus the Christ. After he used a number of Old Testament quotations, he made clear his conclusion.

> Therefore let all the house of Israel know for certain that God has made Him both *Lord and Christ*—this Jesus whom you crucified (Acts 2:36).

As Peter moved to another area of the temple, he had another opportunity to stress Jesus.

> The God of Abraham, Isaac, and Jacob, the God of our fathers, has glorified *His servant Jesus*, the one whom you delivered up, and disowned in the presence of Pilate, when he had decided to release Him. But you disowned the Holy and Righteous One, and asked for a murderer to be granted to you, but put to death the *Prince of life*, the one whom God raised from the dead, a fact to which we are witnesses (Acts 3:13-15).

61

On the next day Peter had a chance to speak to the rulers and elders of the people (Acts 4:8). The subject and focal point of his preaching was the name.

> Let it be known to all of you, and to all the people of Israel, that by the name of Jesus Christ the Nazarene whom you crucified, whom God raised from the dead—by this name the man stands before you in good health (Acts 4:10).

When his activities took him before the council, Peter's sermon did not change.

> The God of our fathers raised up Jesus, whom you had put to death by hanging Him on a cross. He is the one whom God exalted to His right hand as a Prince and a Savior, to grant repentance to Israel, and forgiveness of sins (Acts 5:30-31).

Acts 8 put the spotlight on the preaching of Philip. As he went to a city in Samaria, the subject of his preaching was Christ.

> Philip went down to a city of Samaria, and proclaimed to them *the Christ* (Acts 8:5, RSV).

When he was given the opportunity to teach the man from Ethiopia, he started with Jesus.

> And Philip opened his mouth, and beginning from this Scripture *he preached Jesus* to him (Acts 8:35).

The stress on Jesus as the focal point of one's discipleship continued as the book of Acts unfolded. Peter was given the responsibility of sharing Christ for the first time with the Gentiles in Acts 10. As he did in Acts 2 with the Jews, he placed Jesus at the center of his preaching (Acts 10:34-43).

There are many other examples in Acts of stressing Jesus as the one who merits our following. This stress is not an invention of the early disciples, but something they learned from Jesus as He challenged them to follow Him.

2. Practiced Evangelism

Evangelism was the heart of the first century church. With 3000 converts (Acts 2:41) for a beginning, increase was on a daily basis (Acts 2:47; 5:14; 16:5). Jerusalem was filled with the teaching (Acts 5:28) and a consistent daily preaching program was conducted.

And every day, in the temple and from house to house, *they kept right on teaching and preaching Jesus* as the Christ (Acts 5:42).

Persecution became a blessing in disguise because the gospel moved into other areas more quickly (Acts 8:4). The scattered Christians did not begin preaching because they had been scattered, but they continued to do scattered what they had done at home; i.e. preaching and teaching. Sometimes I hear Christians say that if they went to a mission field, they would be evangelistic. You do not make a missionary out of someone just because you send him across the nation or across the ocean. It is true that it is easier to be evangelistic in the proper atmosphere, but disciples need to be so committed that they create the atmosphere of evangelism.

The gospel spread in the area of Samaria through the efforts of Philip (Acts 8:1-5). Persecution took the word to Phoenicia, Cyprus and Antioch with effective results (Acts 11:21 and 23-26). The gospel took on a world-wide perspective when the church in Antioch sent out Paul and Barnabas (Acts 13:1-3).

It is no surprise that the heart of the early church was evangelism. The great heart of Jesus (a reflection of His Father) yearned for the harvest of souls (John 4:35) and to that end called men into service (Mark 1:17) as fishers. The evangelistic thrust of the early church was carrying out the purpose for which they had been called.

The modern church has adopted the philosophy of trying to get the world to come to a building at a certain time. Too many times evangelistic outreach has started with a building rather than people. The building has become a trap for all the seed that needs to be sown in the world. We have bounced enough seed off the four walls of church buildings to plant the world with the gospel. We must get out where the people are just as the early church did.

3. Endured Losses

Following God in any era has not been without a price. Sacrificing to follow Christ is always a part of the price. Great men and women of God were willing to endure because of the importance of their relationship with God (Hebrews 11:24-26, 32-39).

Some of the losses experienced by the early church to follow Jesus were of a voluntary nature.

And they began selling their property and possessions, and were sharing with all, as anyone might have need. And day by day continuing with one mind in the temple, and breaking bread from house to house, they were taking their meals together with gladness and sincerity of heart (Acts 2:44-45).

And the congregation of those who believed were of one heart and soul; *and not one of them claimed that anything belonging to him was his own; but all things were common property to them.* And with great power the apostles were giving witness to the resurrection of the Lord Jesus, and abundant grace was upon them all. For there was *not a needy person among them,* for all who were owners of land or houses would sell them and bring the proceeds of the sales and lay them at the apostles' feet; and *they would be distributed to each, as any had need* (Acts 4:32-35).

Other early disciples experienced involuntary losses because they chose to follow Jesus. Some of the losses included life (Acts 7:60; 12:1-2); imprisonment (Acts 8:3); stoning (Acts 14:19); beating (Acts 16:23); and a general disrespect for what the early church was.

But we desire to hear from you what your views are; for concerning this sect, it is known to us that *it is spoken against everywhere* (Acts 28:22).

At the end of the first missionary journey, Paul returned to some of the cities to prepare them for future opposition (Acts 14:21-22). Paul prepared the early church for the price of discipleship as Jesus had done with His early followers (Mark 10:29-30; 13:9).

4. Faithfully Proclaimed Christ

The fidelity and faithfulness of the church in Acts in face of discouragement and opposition is a joy to behold. They kept on preaching in spite of imprisonment, threats and losses of all kinds. They could not be kept from proclaiming what they had seen and heard (Acts 4:20). Acts closes with imprisoned Paul preaching the kingdom of God (Acts 28:30-31).

Some of the secular leaders of the day thought they could stop the church's progress by keeping it from meeting. However, you cannot stop an army of soldiers who cannot be bought, intimidated or annihilated. This early church had a determination and a singleness of mind that led them to victory after victory. This attitude is a far cry from a church membership that will allow a little adverse weather or visiting relatives keep them from assembling with the saints.

Chapter 10

Thessalonian Church

Paul gave instructions to the young preachers (Timothy and Titus) about how they were to be evangelistic and were to assist brethren in growing as disciples. The work Paul did in Thessalonica was his laboratory for discipling methods. The church at Thessalonica was the visual aid to show how it should be done and what each individual congregation should be like.

1. Imitated Jesus

The beginning of the church in Thessalonica is found in Acts 17:1-4. The centrality of the preaching was shown in Luke's account of the beginning.

> And according to Paul's custom, he went to them, and for three Sabbaths reasoned with them from the Scriptures, explaining and giving evidence that the Christ had to suffer and rise again from the dead, and saying, *'This Jesus whom I am proclaiming to you is the Christ'* (Acts 17:2-3).

With the background of the church explained in Acts, it is no wonder that Jesus became the model for them to follow. Paul made it clear that the Thessalonians "mimicked" or imitated the Lord.

> You also became *imitators of us and of the Lord*, having received the word in much tribulation with the joy of the Holy Spirit (1 Thessalonians 1:6).

Paul understood that Jesus was the model to follow, but he knew that he was the visual aid for the model.

> Be imitators of me, just as I also am of Christ (1 Corinthians 11:1).

> Not because we do not have the right to do this, but in order to *offer ourselves as a model for you*, that you might follow *our example* (2 Thessalonians 3:9).

Following in the footsteps of Jesus (1 Peter 2:21) is easier when a live example is supplied. It would be difficult for a young Christian to stand firm in the Lord (1 Thessalonians 3:8) without an example of how to stand firm. Not only did Paul realize he was an example of the Lord, but he also urged the young Christians to follow him (Philippians 3:17; 4:9). Unless the young disciple imitates the life of Jesus, his chances for great growth are slim. As you grow in the grace and knowledge of the Lord (2 Peter 3:18), the changes in your lifestyle become evident.

The growth of the church at Thessalonica can be traced to the emphasis on Jesus. Jesus predicted that this growth would take place.

> And I, if I be lifted up from the earth, will draw all men to Myself (John 12:32).

Jesus cannot be the source of growth if He is not preached. It appears that most churches have left the teaching of Jesus to Sunday School classes and have preached the epistles in the pulpit. The pulpit that preaches more of Paul than Jesus has a problem of balance.

2. Evangelized Everywhere

The disciples at Thessalonica took to heart the importance of following the example of Jesus, and, in time, became examples to others. The example of the Lord as an evangelist was known to all, and in turn their example in evangelism became known by all.

> So that you became an example to all the believers in Macedonia and in Achaia. For the world of the Lord has sounded forth from you, not only in Macedonia and Achaia, but also *in every place your faith toward God has gone forth,* so that we have no need to say anything (1 Thessalonians 1:7-8).

What a great example and challenge the Thessalonian church was to the early disciples. The fervor of their zeal and demonstration of their faith served as an impetus for the work in many places.

It is impossible for a disciple to say that he is an imitator of the Lord and not be interested in sounding forth the message as a fisher of men. When a congregation follows Jesus, it will go into all the world with the message. How can a church be Christ-centered when it does not have sharing the message at the heart of all its activities? Christ is depicted as one trying to get into churches who believe they are his.

> Behold, I stand at the door and knock; if anyone hears My voice and opens the door, I will come in to him, and will dine with him, and he with Me (Revelation 3:20).

66

When a church loses its fervor for evangelism, the future cannot be good. The church is writing its own obituary when its attention is turned inward. The preacher for this type of church must take the role of an "undertaker preacher," which is a preacher that is trying to make a dead church look alive!

3. Relationship Toward the World

There are a number of passages which indicate the great price paid by the Thessalonians for discipleship. Paul described their initial reception of the Word as one with much tribulation.

> You also became imitators of us and of the Lord, having *received the word in much tribulation* with the joy of the Holy Spirit (1 Thessalonians 1:6).

Their conversion involved turning from idols to serving the true and living God.

> For they themselves report about us what kind of a reception we had with you, and how *you turned to God from idols* to serve a living and true God (1 Thessalonians 1:9).

This turning involved developing new habits, new ways and new friendships. Breaking with old friends was not easy. It was not inconceivable that opposition and humiliation would come from the idolatrous community.

> For you, brethren, became imitators of the churches of God in Christ Jesus that are in Judea, for *you also endured the same sufferings* at the hands of your own countrymen, even as they did from the Jews (1 Thessalonians 2:14).

The Thessalonians were admonished to expect opposition because of their new direction.

> So that no man may be disturbed by these afflictions, for you yourselves know that we have been destined for this (1 Thessalonians 3:3).

You demonstrate the genuineness of your conversion by a transformed life. Conversion demands the denial of any other "gods." The idols are not only ones of stone and wood, but also attitudes toward this world's goods. Greed can be equaled to idolatry.

> Therefore consider the members of your earthly body as

dead to immorality, impurity, passion, evil desire, and *greed, which amounts to idolatry* (Colossians 3:5).

In BE FREE, Warren W. Wiersbe defines idolatry:

We are to worship God, love people, and use things, but too many times we use people, love self, worship things, and leave God out of the picture completely.[3]

Whatever we worship, we serve.

To make the real break with the world demands a new heart. The disciple approaches his life as one that is not really a part of this world (Colossians 2:20). In turning to God, the Thessalonians were able to make a real impact in their area as a transformed body of believers. The Thessalonians broke with the traditions of the world when they turned to God. You will also break with the traditions of man if your allegiance is to God. Jesus demonstrated this in a discussion with the Pharisees and scribes.

Then some Pharisees and scribes came to Jesus from Jerusalem, saying, 'Why do Your disciples transgress the tradition of the elders? For they do not wash their hands when they eat bread.' And He answered and said to them, 'And why do you yourselves transgress the commandment of God for the sake of your tradition?' (Matthew 15:1-3).

4. Ready for the Coming of Christ

The second coming of Christ is alluded to many times in 1 Thessalonians. Paul was excited about the second coming for the sake of the Thessalonians. He knew they were ready. They were his hope, joy and crown.

For who is our hope or joy or crown of exultation? Is it not even you, in the glory of our Lord, Jesus at His coming? For you are our glory and joy (1 Thessalonians 2:19-20).

In spite of their afflictions and problems they kept their faith and love.

But now that Timothy has come to us from you, and has brought us good news of your faith and love, and that you always think kindly of us, longing to see us just we

[3]Warren W. Wiersbe, BE FREE. (Wheaton, Illinois: Victor Books), 1975, p. 31.

also long to see you (1 Thessalonians 3:6).

Paul was not only confident of his salvation, but also of their salvation.

> For God has not destined us for wrath, but for obtaining
> salvation through our Lord Jesus Christ, who died for us,
> that whether we are awake or asleep, we may live
> together with Him (1 Thessalonians 5:9-10).

The type of discipleship envisioned by Jesus is borne out in the life of this great church. Their faithfulness was not only a joy to Paul, but pleasing to the Lord. Following Jesus is started with a plan to complete. It is not God's intent for anyone to start and not complete the journey. The Thessalonian church stands as an example of God's intent for every congregation. Paul gave the young preachers an example of how to lead a congregation into full maturity. Full maturity is the goal of ministry (Colossians 1:28, NIV).

Chapter 11

Paul

Other than Jesus, no one in the first century made a greater impact for good than Paul. The life of Paul is as well-known as the life of Jesus. The accomplishments of the Hebrew Pharisee from Tarsus have served as a challenge for centuries. Paul's life has served as a model for many "Timothys" to follow.

1. Followed Jesus

Once Paul came to the realization that Jesus was the Christ, he adopted the attitude of obedience to what Jesus wanted for his life.

> And I said, 'What shall I do, Lord?' And the Lord said to
> me, 'Arise and go into Damascus; and there you will be
> told of all that has been appointed for you to do" (Acts
> 22:10).

It was this obedient attitude toward the Lordship of Christ that permeated every decision of his life from that moment on. When Paul was commanded to be baptized by God's preacher, Ananias, there was not a moment's hesitation.

And now why do you delay? Arise, and be baptized, and wash away your sins, calling on His name (Acts 22:16).

As Paul sought to define what life was, he did so in terms of Christ. For Paul, life was Christ and death meant living with Him.

For to me, to live is Christ, and to die is gain (Philippians 1:21).

The prize which Paul sought was found in Christ.

I press on toward the goal for the prize of the upward call of God *in Christ Jesus* (Philippians 3:14).

The cross of Christ became the instrument by which Paul obtained new relationships. As Paul struggled in Galatians with the problem of legalism, he knew the answer was found in Christ. The cross of Christ brought death to self.

I have been *crucified with Christ*; and it is no longer I who live, but Christ lives in me; and the life which I now live in the flesh I live by faith in the Son of God, who loved me, and delivered Himself up for me (Galatians 2:20).

Paul knew that the self-centered life was the off-centered life.

The cross of Christ brought death to the flesh. You do not simply put sin in hibernation; you kill it.

Now those who belong to Christ Jesus *have crucified the flesh* with its passions and desires (Galations 5:24).

The cross brought death to the world. It takes a crucified servant to serve a crucified Lord.

But may it never be that I should boast, except in the cross of our Lord Jesus Christ, through which the *world has been crucified to me*, and I to the world (Galatians 6:14).

Paul knew there could be no discipleship for him or for anyone else unless Christ was the focal point. This great truth was a part of his life and was communicated in the sermons he delivered and in the letters he wrote.

The transformation of this man was unbelievable even to those in the church.

And when he had come to Jerusalem, he was trying to

associate with the disciples; and they were all afraid of him, not believing that he was a disciple (Acts 9:26).

Who would have ever believed that the great antagonist would become the great evangelist. The scourge of the church would become the surge of the church. The Hebrew of Hebrews would become the Christian of Christians. The great change came as a result of one proud Pharisee who said openly and honestly that he wanted to follow Jesus.

It was Jesus Christ who was able to take a proud Pharisee and get him to see that all men are the same in Christ.

There is neither Jew nor Greek, there is neither slave nor free man, there is neither male nor female; for you are all one in Christ Jesus (Galatians 3:28).

The prejudice of his life was not destroyed by governmental declarations, but by a Lord that died for all men.

2. Gave His Life to Evangelism

Paul's ministry was one that was synonymous with evangelism. Jesus' mission to seek and to save the lost (Luke 19:10) had no greater demonstration in anyone more than Paul. The study of Acts is the commentary on this great man's desire to be a fisher of men.

He was willing to evangelize in the very city where he came to seek out and to destroy the Christians. This great desire led him from one life threatening situation to the next. The missionary activities of Acts bear witness to the man's desire for others' salvation. His expression of self-denial is seen in his desire to see his people saved.

I am telling the truth in Christ, I am not lying, my conscience bearing witness in the Holy Spirit, that I have great sorrow and unceasing grief in my heart. For I could wish that I myself were accursed, separated from Christ for the sake of my brethren, my kinsmen according to the flesh (Romans 9:1-3).

Paul not only wanted to give his life to evangelism, but he also wanted to train others to do the same. Through the ones he trained, still others heard the message.

And this took place for two years, so that all who lived in Asia heard the word of the Lord, both Jews and Greeks (Acts 19:10).

71

Paul's pattern in Acts 19:10 followed closely the one established by Jesus.

> And it came about that when Jesus had finished giving instructions to His twelve disciples, He departed from there to teach and to preach in their cities (Matthew 11:1).

In his zeal as a non-Christian, Paul persecuted Christians in foreign cities (Acts 26:11), but as a Christian he took the *gospel* to foreign cities. He expressed his desire to go to Rome.

> For I long to see you in order that I may impart some spiritual gift to you, that you may be established (Romans 1:11).

He knew that the ability to take the gospel around the world was not his but Christ working in him.

> For I will not presume to speak of anything except what Christ has accomplished through me, resulting in the obedience of the Gentiles by word and deed, in the power of signs and wonders, in the power of the Spirit; *so that from Jerusalem and around about as far as Illyricum I have fully preached the gospel of Christ* (Romans 15:18-19).

Paul had a goal to take the gospel to Spain.

> Therefore when I have finished this, and have put my seal on this fruit of theirs, I will go on by way of you to Spain (Romans 15:28).

According to secular evidence he achieved his goal. Clement of Rome, who lived during the latter part of the first century, declared that Paul had preached to the end of the known world (1 Clement 5:6 and 7).

3. Gave Up Earthly Gain

Very few men have paid the price Paul paid to follow Jesus. As a leading Pharisee he had a secure future in front of him, but he felt that knowing Christ was far more important.

> Although I myself might have confidence even in the flesh. If anyone else has a mind to put confidence in the flesh, I far more; circumcised the eighth day, of the nation of Israel, of the tribe of Benjamin, a Hebrew of

Hebrews; as to the law, a Pharisee; as to zeal, a persecutor of the church; as to the righteousness which is in the Law, found blameless. But whatever things were gain to me, those things I have counted as loss for the sake of Christ. More than that, I count all things to be loss in view of the surpassing value of knowing Christ Jesus my Lord, for whom I have suffered the loss of all things, and count them but rubbish in order that I may gain Christ, and may be found in Him, not having righteousness of my own derived from the Law, but that which is through faith in Christ, the righteousness which comes from God on the basis of faith, that I may know Him, and the power of His resurrection and the fellowship of His sufferings, being conformed to His death; in order that I may attain to the resurrection from the dead (Philippians 3:4-11).

The physical abuse Paul suffered served as a great incentive for faithfulness in the lives of others. The book of Acts is filled with examples of the price Paul paid to be an evangelist. As Paul wrote his personal manual on ministry, he gave a compact statement on his personal cost of discipleship.

Are they servants of Christ? (I speak as if insane) I more so; in far more labors, in far more imprisonments, beaten times without number, often in danger of death. Five times I received from the Jews thirty-nine lashes. Three times I was beaten with rods, once I was stoned, three times I was shipwrecked, a night and a day I have spent in the deep. I have been on frequent journeys, in dangers from rivers, dangers from robbers, dangers from my countrymen, dangers from the Gentiles, dangers in the city, dangers in the wilderness, dangers on the sea, dangers among false brethren; I have been in labor and hardship, through many sleepless nights, in hunger and thirst, often without food, in cold and exposure. Apart from such external things, there is the daily pressure upon me of concern for all the churches (2 Corinthians 11:23-28).

We will never know how many young men were encouraged to stay faithful knowing the price Paul paid to serve Jesus.

4. Faithful to the End

As we read the story of Paul in Acts for the first time, excitement builds, anticipating the outcome of this great man's life. There is something of a letdown when we realize a final chapter was not written on him. However, his faithfulness in the face of such opposition is a wonder to behold.

The enemies of Paul continued to follow him in order to make trouble for him.

> And when the seven days were almost over, the Jews from Asia, upon seeing him in the temple, began to stir up all the multitude and laid hands on him (Acts 21:27).

Because of the problems created by his enemies, he was arrested (Acts 21:28-40). In the face of the angry mob, Paul didn't want to miss a chance to share Christ with them. When a desire for self-preservation might have taken over Paul's actions, he showed that he was not ashamed of his faith or belief in the risen Savior. This type of attitude became his trademark through the imprisonment in Rome.

After making an outstanding defense by relating his conversion, he saw an opportunity to demonstrate his faithfulness to Christ and told the story to the council. However, Paul saw that he would not get a fair hearing and chose to confuse the meeting.

> But perceiving that one part were Sadducees and the other Pharisees, Paul began crying out in the Council, 'Brethren, I am a Pharisee, a son of Pharisees; I am on trial for the hope and resurrection of the dead!' And as he said this, there arose a dissension between the Pharisees and the Sadducees; and the assembly was divided (Acts 23:6-7).

As a result of this move, a great dissension developed and he was taken to a more secure place (Acts 23:9-10). The activities of Paul up to this point demanded faith and courage. It is interesting to note that the Lord confirmed to Paul that he was doing the right things and that he would eventually make it to Rome.

> But on the night immediately following, the Lord stood at his side and said, 'Take courage; for as you have solemnly witnessed to My cause at Jerusalem, so you must witness at Rome also' (Acts 23:11).

Jesus sought to prepare His disciples for what would happen to them because of their allegiance to Him. It was difficult for this band of fishermen to really envision what lay ahead of them. Before Jesus was brought before kings and governors because of His faithfulness to His Father, He told His disciples to get ready for the same treatment.

> But before all these things, they will lay their hands on you and will persecute you, delivering you to the synagogues and prisons, bringing you before kings and governors for My name's sake. It will lead to an opportunity for your testimony. So make up your minds not to prepare beforehand to defend yourselves (Luke 21:12-14).

This type of treatment should not be considered all bad because it will give you an opportunity to share the basis of your faith. This type of preparation of His disciples was also demonstrated in the life of Paul. His defenses of the Christian faith before Felix the governor (Acts 24:1-4) and Agrippa the king (Acts 26:1-2) are classic examples of faithfulness and courage.

In his defense before Felix, he gave an account of what had taken place in order to explain the events of the hour (Acts 24:1-21). However, Paul did not let this great opportunity to convert a government leader go by. The subject of his sermon to Felix was his faith in Christ Jesus (Acts 24:24). Luke preserved for the reader the heart of his discussion and the response to the message.

> And as he was discussing righteousness, self-control and the judgment to come, Felix became frightened and said, 'Go away for the present, and when I find time, I will summon you' (Acts 24:25).

The dangerous trip to Rome did not dampen his faithfulness to proclaim the message. Paul had confidence that his God would deliver him. When Paul used his own knowledge of the situation, he believed that there would be a loss of cargo, ship and lives (Acts 27:10). However, God told Paul how it would really be.

> And yet now I urge you to keep up your courage, for there shall be no loss of life among you, but only of the ship. For this very night an angel of the God *to whom I belong* and *whom I serve stood* before me, saying, 'Do not be afraid, Paul; you must stand before Caesar; and behold, God has granted you all those who are sailing with you' (Acts 27:22-24).

Paul stated that this was the God to whom he *belonged* and whom he *served*. When a disciple knows to whom he belongs and whom he serves, faithfulness will be the result! Paul had so much confidence in the word of his God that he said:

> Therefore, keep up your courage, men, for I believe God, that it will turn out exactly as I have been told (Acts 27:25).

Luke concluded the book of Acts with a summary of Paul's activities.

> And he stayed two full years in his own rented quarters, and was welcoming all who came to him, preaching the kingdom of God and teaching concerning the Lord Jesus Christ with all openness, unhindered (Acts 28:30-31).

The effectiveness of Paul's preaching from the time of his arrest to his imprisonment in Rome cannot be fully measured; however, some of Caesar's household were converted either during the trip to Rome or after his arrival. This truth was demonstrated when he wrote to the brethren in Philippi.

> Greet every saint in Christ Jesus. The brethren who are with me greet you. All the saints greet you, especially those of Caesar's household (Philippians 4:21-22).

It appears that Paul was released from the imprisonment mentioned at the close of Acts. Some have thought that he went to Spain between the imprisonment of Acts 28:30-31 and the one discussed in 2 Timothy. The 2 Timothy imprisonment seemed to be more confining than the one in Acts. There is a possibility that his treatment changed from the close of Acts to the writing of 2 Timothy, but this is doubtful. When he wrote the prison epistles (Philippians, Ephesians, Philemon and Colossians), there was the anticipation and hope of being released. The 2 Timothy imprisonment continued to demonstrate his faithfulness to the cause of Christ. He summarized his life and spoke confidently of the future.

> For I am already being poured out as a drink offering, and the time of my departure has come. I have fought the good fight, I have finished the course, I have kept the faith; in the future there is laid up for me the crown of righteousness, which the Lord, the righteous Judge, will award to me on that day; and not only to me, but also to all who have loved His appearing (2 Timothy 4:6-8).

However, what was even more amazing about the faithfulness of this great disciple was his desire to be a student to the very end.

> When you come bring the cloak which I left at Troas with Carpus, and the books, especially the parchments (2 Timothy 4:13).

Perhaps it is because there is so much material on Paul, but there is no greater example of the purpose that God has for His followers. Everything that Jesus wants in His disciples was found in Paul. The number of lives this type of following touched in Paul's lifetime and in the many lifetimes to follow can never be known.

Chapter 12

Barnabas

Other than Jesus Christ, there was no other man who had a greater influence on the life of Paul than Barnabas. After Paul's conversion, it was Barnabas who explained the situation to the disciples in Jerusalem.

> And when he had come to Jerusalem, he was trying to associate with the disciples; and they were all afraid of him, not believing that he was a disciple. But Barnabas took hold of him and brought him to the apostles and described to them how he had seen the Lord on the road, and that He had talked to him, and how at Damascus he had spoken out boldly in the name of Jesus (Acts 9:26-27).

After Barnabas was sent to the young church in Antioch, he realized he needed more help.

> And the hand of the Lord was with them, and a large number who believed turned to the Lord. And the news about them reached the ears of the church at Jerusalem, and they sent Barnabas off to Antioch. Then when he had come and witnessed the grace of God, he rejoiced and began to encourage them with all resolute heart to remain true to the Lord; for he was a good man, and full of the Holy Spirit and of faith. And considerable numbers were brought to the Lord. *And he left for Tarsus to look for Saul;* and when he had found him he brought him to

Antioch. And it came about that for an entire year they met with the church, and taught considerable numbers; and the disciples were first called Christians in Antioch (Acts 11:21-26).

This was an important point in the life of Paul because it was soon after this that Paul and Barnabas embarked on the first missionary journey (Acts 13:1-2). It would appear that Paul was in a semi-seclusion and Barnabas brought him into the arena of his life. Paul was seeking to be a follower of Christ (1 Corinthians 11:1), and the life of Barnabas was a good example to follow. I wonder if Paul would have ever been the great apostle to the Gentiles had it not been for the interest and example of Barnabas. Barnabas showed what a real servant was in his dealings with Paul.

1. True to the Lord

Of all the men in the church in Jerusalem who could have been sent to a new work, the church selected Barnabas to go. Part of the reason for his selection could be traced back to the type of person he was. His original name was not Barnabas, but Joseph. Because of the kind of person he was, his name was changed by the apostles to one that meant Son of Encouragement (Acts 4:36). When a good man—who is full of the Holy Spirit, faith, rejoicing at the grace of God—urges disciples to remain true to the Lord, there can be little doubt as to what the outcome will be—"considerable numbers were brought to the Lord" (Acts 11:24).

Barnabas showed the source of his true commitment to be Jesus Christ when he, in turn, urged the same for their lives. He knew from experience the need to have this direction if spiritual growth were to become a reality. With this type of emphasis at the beginning of the church in Antioch, it was destined to be a church with great missionary zeal. How could a church remain true to the Lord and not true to the very mission of the Lord? Following the Lord will be demonstrated as you follow the mission of the Lord.

2. Missionary Work

The missionary zeal which brought Barnabas from Jerusalem to Antioch provided the basis for him to be sent into all the world. Barnabas proved himself to be a fisher of men in Antioch. There was little doubt in the minds of the leaders at Antioch that he would do the same thing as a companion to Paul in the first great missionary journey. Barnabas' dedication and commitment to carry the message to unknown places is told in Acts 13-14. He was faithful in his proclamation and encouraged Paul to do the same thing. It appeared that because of his commitment to the Lord, that being involved in evangelistic work is unquestioned. Evangelism is a natural expression of your being true to the Lord.

3. Sold Possessions

The beginning of the church in Jerusalem in the second chapter of Acts must have produced excitement beyond description. It must have been great to witness three thousand people becoming disciples of Jesus, with the number increasing on a daily basis (Acts 2:41 and 47). The original trip to Jerusalem for most was not in order to become followers of Jesus, but to observe an annual Jewish feast day. In order to accommodate the needs of these new disciples who wanted to stay longer to learn more about what it meant to be a follower of Jesus, an emergency collection of goods was taken.

> And all those who had believed were together, and had all things in common; and they began selling their property and possessions, and were sharing them with all, as anyone might have need (Acts 2:44-45).

It appears that Barnabas was among the early converts in the beginning of the church. Continual growth was characteristic of the church from the very beginning.

> But many of those who had heard the message believed; and the number of the men came to be about *five thousand* (Acts 4:4).

Barnabas chose to participate in meeting the physical needs of all these new disciples.

> And the congregation of those who believed were of one heart and soul; and not one of them claimed that anything belonging to him was his own; but all things were common property to them. And with great power the apostles were giving witness to the resurrection of the Lord Jesus, and abundant grace was upon them all. For there was not a needy person among them, for all who were owners of land or houses would sell them and bring the proceeds of the sales, and lay them at the apostles' feet; and they would be distributed to each, as any had need. And Joseph, a Levite of Cyprian birth, who was also called Barnabas by the apostles (which translated

means, Son of Encouragement), and who owned a tract
of land, sold it and brought the money and laid it at the
apostles' feet (Acts 4:32-37).

Barnabas knew that the new relationship he had with God through
the Lord Jesus Christ was brought about with great expense on the
part of God and Jesus; therefore, he was willing to sacrifice
whatever he could as an expression of his appreciation for his new
redemption. When one is owned by God, it is not difficult to give
away what he has since he understands that it is not his to keep.

This type of generosity became commonplace in the life of the early church. Paul described this type of sacrifice when he wrote to the
church at Corinth (2 Corinthians 8:1-5). Deep poverty does not
keep one from giving liberally. Even though he was a sacrificing
disciple, Paul was amazed that these poverty-ridden disciples gave
more than he anticipated. The factor in their giving was the same
key factor as in Barnabas' giving—giving one's self to the Lord. The
heart of giving is the giving of the heart. When one has not really
committed himself to following Jesus, giving will always be a problem. After Paul told of the sacrificial giving by the churches in
Macedonia, he urged Corinth (located to the south of Macedonia in
Achaia) to remember what Jesus had done.

For you know the grace of our Lord Jesus Christ, that
though He was rich, yet for your sake He became poor,
that you through His poverty might become rich
(2 Corinthians 8:9).

The motivation for sacrifice can always be traced back to the
sacrifice of Jesus.

4. Preached in Cyprus in Later Years

The first missionary journey Barnabas took with Paul was a great
success. Some areas were more fruitful than others, but the overall
results were a thrill to all who heard their report.

And after they had preached the gospel to that city and
had made many disciples, they returned to Lystra and to
Iconium and to Antioch, strengthening the souls of the
disciples, encouraging them to continue in the faith, and
saying, 'Through many tribulations we must enter the
kingdom of God.' . . . And when they had arrived and
gathered the church together, they began to report all

things that God had done with them and how He had opened a door of faith to the Gentiles (Acts 14:21-22,27).

With the successful evangelistic efforts among the Gentiles, some problems arose. Acts 15 is a description of the events surrounding the solution to these related problems. A letter was sent out to everyone telling of the decision that was made (Acts 15:22-29). With this major problem behind them, Paul suggested to Barnabas a need to visit some of the brethren where they had just preached to see how they were doing (Acts 15:36). Barnabas was in favor of going, but he wanted to take John Mark along with them. Paul did not agree with this suggestion because John Mark had left them on the first journey (Acts 15:37-38). There was such a sharp disagreement between Paul and Barnabas over whether or not John Mark should go on the second trip that Paul and Barnabas separated from one another. Instead of making a big issue of the disagreement, Paul chose Silas, and Barnabas chose Mark and the two groups went their separate ways to fulfill the mission of Jesus (Acts 15:39-31.)

It would be difficult to calculate the age of Barnabas at the time he took John Mark and went to Cyprus, but a guess of the early 60's would be reasonable. Barnabas was old enough to have lands to be sold in the early days of the church (Acts 4:36-37). The time of the trip to Cyprus would have been approximately 20 years after the beginning of the church. At an age when most would be thinking about their retirement years of leisure, Barnabas was carrying the burden of the lost of his home country. He was not content with spending his last years where there were many disciples, but his missionary spirit urged him to be faithful to the great commission of going into all the world until the day of his death.

Barnabas' faithfulness had a lasting effect on John Mark's life. The original confidence that Paul had in John Mark to take him on the first missionary tour was restored because of the efforts and faithfulness of Barnabas. In Paul's last imprisonment, he expressed his loneliness because of some of his departed fellow laborers, such as Demas. As he wrote to Timothy, he urged him to bring John Mark with him when he came to visit.

Only Luke is with me. Pick up Mark and bring him with you, for he is useful to me for service (2 Timothy 4:11).

Barnabas' faithfulness as a disciple had a profound effect on individuals (Paul and John Mark) and areas (Antioch and Cyprus). What God is able to do through the life of one committed disciple is amazing and unbelievable. Barnabas will live on forever as an example of one who committed himself in the early days of the church to a life of evangelism, sacrifice and faithfulness to the end.

His effectiveness was enhanced more by his availability than his ability. This has always been characteristic of God's great servants. Isaiah's availability to the will of God serves as a challenge to all who will follow.

> Then I heard the voice of the Lord, saying, 'Whom shall I send and who will go for Us?' Then I said, *'Here am I, send me!'* (Isaiah 6:8).

The reluctance of the prophet Amos to go north and prophesy is well known.

> Then Amos answered and said to Amaziah, *'I am not a prophet, nor am I the son of a prophet;* for I am a herdsman and a grower of sycamore figs' (Amos 7:14).

In both of these cases their mission was accomplished because of their availability. It is not only the five-talent disciple that God can use effectively but also the disciple who is willing to make the kind of commitment that it will take to change the whole world.

Conclusion

God's original purpose for His people has now come to light in the life of the church and in the lives of the individual disciples. With the eternal purpose being the salvation of the world and the glorification of God, what greater way could these purposes be fulfilled than in the lives of dedicated disciples? Demonstration and transformation are core concepts in the mind of God. God has never been interested in external sacrifice more than in the personal sacrifice of one who desires to follow Him (Psalm 51:16-17; Micah 6:6-8). God's purpose has basically been the same throughout the ages—He wants the best that you have to offer, and He wants it all! In order for you to be the best that you can be, you must change and conform to His image as revealed in Jesus.

The following chart shows the strong correlation in the *demonstration* of discipleship, which is an outgrowth of the *demand* of discipleship, that was patterned after the *design* of discipleship, found in the nature of God and manifested in Jesus:

1. Object of Discipleship
   a. Stressed Christ (Acts 2:36; 3:13-15; 4:10; 5:30-31; 8:5,35;

11:23; 16:15)
   b. Imitated Jesus (1 Thessalonians 1:6)
   c. Followed Jesus (Acts 22:10)
   d. True to the Lord (Acts 11:23)
2. Purpose of Discipleship
   a. Practiced evangelism (Acts 2:41,47; 5:42; 8:4)
   b. Evangelized everywhere (1 Thessalonians 1:7-8)
   c. Gave his life to evangelism (Acts 19:10)
   d. Missionary work (Acts 13:1-3)
3. Cost of Discipleship
   a. Endured losses (Acts 2:44-45; 14:22)
   b. Relationship toward the world (1 Thessalonians 1:9)
   c. Gave up earthly gain (Philippians 3:4-11)
   d. Sold possessions (Acts 4:32-37)
4. Results of Discipleship
   a. Faithfully proclaimed Christ (Acts 4:20)
   b. Ready for the Coming of Christ (1 Thessalonians 2:19-20)
   c. Faithful to the end (2 Timothy 4:6-8)
   d. Preached in Cyprus in later years (Acts 15:39-41).

These early disciples realized that they were representing God to a lost world. Their major concern was not their own personal reputation and the image of the church, but whether or not they were involved in the eternal purpose of God. The modern church is so concerned about image and reputation that it is afraid to do anything that would upset the community. Disciples need to realize they represent the God of the universe and the King of Kings rather than an institution, school or philosophy. The great commission of Jesus was not to go into all the world and be a good example, watch your influence and guard your reputation, but to preach the gospel to all the nations! This does not mean that disciples should not be concerned with their influence and reputation, but that it cannot be allowed to be a hindrance to taking the message to those who need it. Had the modern church been thriving in the first century, how would they have reacted to Paul's evangelistic methods of going to the scum of the earth? The church in the first century was either loved or hated, but it was not treated with indifference.

When communicable diseases were rampant in our country, the solution to controlling epidemics was to isolate the carriers. Some of the diseases that used to plague this country were conquered in this manner. The devil attempts to use the same method in the church today. If the carriers of the gospel can be limited to a few "professionally trained preachers," and these men can be herded into a building and made into highly paid office boys, he has won the victory against the Lord! Until we can restore in the life of every disciple an allegiance to Christ that supercedes all other commitments, a burning desire to help others become what he has become by the grace of God, and a willingness to sacrifice whatever needs to be given to get the job done, the eternal purpose of God to save the world will never become a reality.

The early church did not face a very pretty world, and the world the 20th century disciple faces is not much better. The courage to face a sin-filled world comes from the reality of an empty tomb, a risen Lord and an approach to life that makes sense when nothing else does. Even with an uncertain future the disciple lives with confidence knowing that because God lives he can face tomorrow. One song says, "Because I know all fear is gone, and He holds the future, and life is worth living because He lives." When the world is in turmoil and trouble, the disciple can have a peace which the world cannot give.

> Peace I leave with you; My peace I give to you; not as the world gives, do I give to you. Let not your heart be troubled, nor let it be fearful (John 14:27).

> The steadfast of mind Thou wilt keep in perfect peace, because he trusts in Thee (Isaiah 26:3).

The peace that Jesus and His Father desires for Their followers is found when you are willing to commit yourself to the task of being a disciple. You must commit yourself to being a part of the family of God.

> For you are all sons of God through faith in Christ Jesus. For all of you who were baptized into Christ have clothed yourselves with Christ (Galatians 3:26-27).

By obedience to the will of God we can become a part of the family of God. This is a commitment that you must make personally. God has sons, but no grandsons. We are Christians by regeneration rather than generation. Discipleship is not inherited. It is brought about by a solemn choice to follow.

Section IV

The Discipleship Test

Sometimes the word "test" brings fear into the lives of people, but the word is not a bad one. A test tells you where your strengths or weaknesses are. It can be a measurement for future changes and work. You will never know how strong you really are unless you are willing to take a test. You can't know your weight unless you are willing to subject yourself to a proven scale. What others perceive you to be, and what you really are, are not necessarily the same. People who are interested in strength or improvement are not afraid of tests but use them as stepping stones to greater improvement.

In the spiritual realm, measurements are important in order to have an accurate assessment of ourselves. Many times the standards that we use to prove our discipleship are not necessarily accurate measurements. Perfect attendance at church services and memorizing scriptures or Biblical facts are good but are not the final proofs of discipleship in the mind of God.

This study has traced the concept of discipleship from the nature of God, through the teachings of Jesus, to its demonstration in the first century. A good measure of one's discipleship in the 20th century could be established by the consideration of four questions devised from the four ideas that have been correlated throughout this study.

Chapter 13

Are You Following Jesus?

There are certain aspects of life which you cannot control.

Whether or not you will be born, the color of your eyes, and how tall you will be are a few examples. However, you do have control over your will which, in turn, determines the direction of your life. There are many competitive forces which demand a following. Men with charisma, religious papers with wide circulation, universities with national prominence, and appealing philosophies are but a few of the possibilities. The true disciple must determine to follow Jesus without respect to men, religious papers, universities or philosophies. The only authority the disciple checks with before he makes a decision is Jesus Christ and God's revealed will. For the disciple, Jesus occupies a position that will not be shared with anyone or anything. When a decision of right or wrong is presented, Christ becomes the ultimate standard of decision. The disciple will not think about giving in to the pressures of the world but will remain true to his commitment to follow Jesus.

The disciple realizes that by following Jesus, he is saying that he is not his own, but is owned by the Master who purchased him with the price of His very own life. When Paul argued against immorality being a part of the Christian's lifestyle, he set forth his case from the standpoint of ownership.

> Or do you not know that your body is a temple of the Holy Spirit who is in you, whom you have from God and that you are not your own? For *you have been bought with a price;* therefore glorify God in your body (1 Corinthians 6:19-20).

The price for the redemption of the disciple was the life of Jesus. Jesus knew the price that He had to pay in order to command the kind of discipleship that God intended for His creation.

> Just as the Son of Man did not come to be served, but to serve, and *to give His life* as a ransom for many (Matthew 20:28).

Around the neck of every disciple hangs an imaginary sign: "Not for sale at any price—bought and paid for at Calvary."

The disciple who is willing to sell out to the highest bidder has never really made the commitment to follow Jesus. One who is willing to be controlled by circumstance rather than principle will find himself selling Jesus for a lot less than Judas did. When the principle of, "I will follow Jesus in all situations," is deeply ingrained, proper decisions will be made in all circumstances of life.

The examples of other disciples of Jesus help in directing your life, but this can *never* be a replacement or substitute for the real Master of your life—Jesus. Following men, such as was the case in Corinth (1 Corinthians 1:12-16), was never the intention of God. The partisan spirit of men-following was not the real problem of the Corinthians, but it was a manifestation of their use of worldly wisdom.

Knowing Jesus is essential in order for you to really follow Him. For this reason, a study of His life with a desire to be like Him in every way is important. How can the disciple follow someone whom he does not know? How can he follow if his knowledge of him is second or third-hand? Instead of simply reading books about Him or hearing sermons which are other's conclusions about Jesus, the disciple should seek to find out for himself more about the Christ he claims to follow. The conclusions and findings of others are helpful but should never be substituted for the disciple's own discovery of the Christ. Jesus does not simply want a great following, but He wants dedicated followers. In a real sense there is a difference in simply following and being a true follower. The religious world has produced some movements which have had a great following without producing genuine followers of the man from Nazareth.

Chapter 14

Are You Working Spiritually in the Lives of Others?

Discipleship in God's eternal purpose does not allow you the luxury of choice when it comes to working in the lives of others. When Jesus gave the Great Commission (Matthew 28:18-20) to make disciples of all nations, it was not so much a command as it was a release for disciples to do what should be natural—to make other disciples. It is natural for you to want others to be like you in attitude, purpose and outlook.

The ministry of Jesus was dedicated to working in the spiritual lives of others. When Jesus chose the apostles, they were far from what Jesus wanted them to be. His success ratio was outstanding (11 out of 12). The transformation that Jesus effected in their lives is a challenge to all. He was able to take one of the sons of Thunder (Mark 3:17) (who sought a place of greatness [Mark 10:35-37], who had no patience or love for people who rejected Jesus [Luke 9:54]) and to turn him into the apostle of love. This same apostle was now willing to assist the same Samaritans that he had wanted to burn to the ground a few years earlier (Acts 8:14-15).

The example of Jesus working in the lives of others was a motivation to Paul. Very seldom did Paul go alone on trips, but he took others with him and in turn was able to work in their lives. Jesus saw the disciples as being "His."

> And you shall say to the owner of the house, 'The teacher
> says to you, "Where is the guest room in which I may eat
> the Passover with *My disciples?*" ' (Luke 22:11).

Paul saw his disciples in a similar way because he referred to Timothy as "my beloved son," (2 Timothy 1:2). The use of "my" does not denote ownership any more than does the reference to "my gospel" (Romans 2:16) indicates ownership. "My" indicates closeness and relationship. The disciple can have "his disciples" without owning them. Everyone has someone who is following him. When the disciple realizes his responsibility to "his disciples," it tends to encourage one to a closer walk with Jesus.

Paul made it clear to Timothy that he had a responsibility to others. Paul gave one of the important keys in the ministry of discipleship.

> And the things which you have heard from me in the
> presence of many witnesses, these entrust to faithful men,
> who will be able to teach others also (2 Timothy 2:2).

Timothy could not be satisfied with only receiving the message from Paul, but he had to give it to faithful men who must not be satisfied with keeping it, but in turn shared it with others. Paul is an example of one who developed others to the extent that they saw spiritual grandchildren in their ministries. The key to world evangelism is not just leading people to Christ but developing them so that they can do the same thing. The disciple needs to be "germinal" and not "terminal" with the message of salvation.

It is not easy to work in the lives of others. It takes time, effort, courage, patience, endurance, consistency and a willingness to risk failure. The ministry of Jesus stands as a monument to the difficulty of working with others. The disappointments will be many. Jesus was disappointed in a young man He loved who was not willing to pay the price to follow.

> And he said to Him, 'Teacher, I have kept all these things
> from my youth up.' And looking at him, *Jesus felt a love
> for him,* and said to him, 'One thing you lack; go and sell

all you possess, and give to the poor, and you shall have treasure in heaven; and come, follow Me.' But at these words his face fell, and *he went away grieved, for he was one who owned much property* (Luke 10:20-22).

The disappointment Paul experienced with his fellow laborer, Demas, must have been heartbreaking (2 Timothy 4:10). What is the difference between the kind of discipleship in which you feel comfortable and self-satisfied and the kind that is characterized by personal cost? The spiritual reproduction of your life in the lives of others. The present day disciples of Jesus need to decide whether they want to be known as fishers of men or simply keepers of the aquarium! If God's eternal purpose for the world is to be fulfilled, it must be executed by the disciples of Jesus. It is God's desire to save the world (2 Peter 3:9; 1 Timothy 2:4). There is no greater way to accomplish God's eternal purpose than for every disciple of Jesus to work in the lives of others to make them disciples of Jesus, who in turn will do that to others.

Chapter 15

Are There Things in Your Life That You Are Not Willing to Surrender in Order to be a Real Disciple?

When you accept Jesus as your leader and guide, it is not without a price. When you decide to follow Jesus, you don't just cut down on your sinning but you get out of the sinning business. The ideal for you is not to sin.

My little children, I am writing these things to you that you may not sin (1 John 2:1a).

However, in spite of the ideal you do sin.

If *we* say that *we* have no sin, *we* are deceiving *ourselves*, and the truth is not in *us*. If *we* confess *our* sins, He is faithful and righteous to forgive *us our* sins and to cleanse *us* from all unrighteousness. If *we* say that *we* have not sinned, *we* make Him a liar, and His word is not in *us* (1 John 1:8-10).

You forfeit the right to sin when you say you are willing to follow Jesus wherever He leads (Luke 9:57). The disciple does not have the right to sin—only the ability. The disciple might rejoice that sins which at one time dominated his life are no longer a part of his life, but he cannot be thoroughly satisfied until all that distracts him from serving the Lord are gone from his life. There is no premium on mediocrity.

When Jesus made disciples of men, He wanted to change their actions as well as their very natures. If their actions are the only alteration—and the nature is not changed—the disciple will lack depth and the power to be everything God intends for him to be. Jesus' teaching from the sermon on the mount (Matthew 5-7) was not intended to solely change actions but the attitudes which produced those actions. Jesus knew the importance of transforming the disciple's inner heart.

> This people honor me with their lips, but their *heart* is far away from me (Matthew 15:8).

> For as he thinks within himself so he is. He says to you, 'Eat and drink!' But his *heart* is not with you (Proverbs 23:7).

Paul took the same approach as he worked with disciples in their practical lives. Paul stressed that without a death, no real discipleship would take place. They had to die to be free from sin.

> For he who has died is freed from sin (Romans 6:7).

There have to be two deaths before discipleship can be real. The first death is the death of Christ. Without His death there can be no accessibility to the Father.

> And He came and preached peace to you who were far away and peace to those who were near; for through Him we both have *access in one Spirit to the Father* (Ephesians 2:17-18).

When you are baptized, you are baptized into the death of Christ.

> Or do you not know that all of us who have been baptized into Christ Jesus have been *baptized into His death?* (Romans 6:3).

At this point the disciple is brought into union with Christ and the benefits of His death are appropriated to the disciple. The second death is the one the disciple experiences when he is brought into union with Christ.

> Therefore we have been *buried with Him through baptism into death,* in order that as Christ was raised from the dead through the glory of the Father, so we too might walk in newness of life. For if we have become *united with Him in the likeness of His death,* certainly we shall be also in the likeness of His resurrection, knowing this, that our *old self was crucified with Him,* that our body of sin might be done away with, that we should *no longer be slaves to sin* (Romans 6:4-6).

After the disciple's death, he can walk in a newness of life, in union with his Lord with the purpose of no longer being a slave to sin. The death of the disciple changes what he is. This will have a great affect on what he does.

> *Now if we have died with Christ,* we believe that we shall also live with Him, knowing that Christ, having been raised from the dead, is never to die again; death no longer is master over Him. For the death that He died, He died to sin, once for all; but the life that He lives, He lives to God. Even so *consider yourselves to be dead to sin,* but alive to God in Christ Jesus. Therefore, *do not let sin reign in your mortal body* that you should obey its lusts, and do not go on presenting the members of your body to sin as instruments of unrighteousness; but present yourselves to God as those alive from the dead, and your members as instruments of righteousness to God. *For sin shall not be master over you,* but you are not under law, but under grace (Romans 6:8-14).

When Paul dealt with sin in the life of the disciple, it stemmed from the fact that a death had taken place in his life.

> If then you have been raised up with Christ, keep seeking the things above, where Christ is seated at the right hand of God. Set your mind on the things above, not on the things that are on earth. *For you have died* and your life is hidden with Christ Jesus (Colossians 3:1-3).

Since the disciple has died, he should put to death sin in his life.

91

> *Put to death*, therefore, whatever belongs to your earthly
> nature: sexual immorality, impurity, lust, evil desires
> and greed, which is idolatry (Colossians 3:5, NIV).

When the disciple eliminates these sins from his life, he is doing (putting to death) out of what he has become (dead). The disciple does not accomplish the complete purpose of God for his life by merely changing his diet, but also his appetite.

Not only must the disciple be willing to surrender the sins of his life with a resolve to live only for the Lord, but also to surrender other things so more people may become followers of Jesus. Paul's complete lifestyle was altered so that others could be saved.

> For though I am free from all men, I have made myself a
> slave to all, that I might win the more. And to the Jews I
> became as a Jew that I might win Jews; to those who are
> under the law, as under the Law, though not being
> myself under the Law, that I might win those who are
> under the Law; to those who are without the law, as
> without the law, though not being without the law of
> God but under the law of Christ, that I might win those
> who are without the law. To the weak, I became weak,
> that I might win the weak! I have become all things to all
> men, that I may be all means save some. And I do all
> things for the sake of the gospel, that I may become a
> fellow partaker of it (1 Corinthians 9:19-23).

Everything Paul did in his life pointed to saving the world. He felt he must do all he could in order for God's eternal purpose to be accomplished in man. He was willing to forego any actions that he deemed right if those actions distracted others from following Jesus.

> For through your knowledge he who is weak is ruined,
> the brother for whose sake Christ died. And thus, by sinning against the brethren and wounding their conscience
> when it is weak, you sin against Christ. Therefore, if food
> causes my brother to stumble, I will never eat meat
> again, that I might not cause my brother to stumble
> (1 Corinthians 8:11-13).

An action might be right in and of itself, but if it in some way hinders making and maturing disciples in the fullness of Christ, the sensitive disciple must give serious consideration to giving it up.

The disciple must have a thirst for holy living because he wants to be like the God he serves. One of the foundation stones for growth is seen in a relationship with the divine.

> For by these he has granted to us His precious and magnificent promises, in order that by them *you might become partakers of the divine nature*, having escaped the corruption that is in the world by lust. Now for this very reason also, applying all diligence, in your faith supply moral excellence, and in your moral excellence, knowledge; and in your knowledge, self-control, and in your self-control, perseverance, and in your perseverance, godliness; and in your godliness, brotherly kindness, and in your brotherly kindness, love. For if these qualities are yours and are increasing, they render you neither useless nor unfruitful in the true knowledge of our Lord Jesus Christ (2 Peter 1:4-8).

When the disciple doesn't realize that he is a partaker in the divine nature, he is missing a key element in his growth pattern. The desire to be an "average disciple" is not possible for one who takes seriously the challenge to follow Jesus.

It is human to measure the value of items by the amount paid for them. We don't get upset if an inexpensive item is lost or destroyed, but items with a high monetary value or one obtained with much hard work and sacrifice is a different story. If the disciple pays relatively nothing to follow, he will not be overly concerned with the importance. In times of choice or decision, he will normally choose that of greater value to him. Without sacrifice or full surrender there cannot be much value placed on his following.

Chapter 16

Is Your Discipleship Present Tense or Past Tense?

You cannot be satisfied with what you used to be or have accomplished. What you are now is crucial. At times, age and infirmities can limit your ability to function at the same capacity and rate of the past, but growing in the likeness of Christ never ends.

It is not God's purpose for men to follow for a short period of time or to get in so many years of Christian service and then retire. He wants His disciples to follow until they are called home to be with Him (Revelation 14:13). The rest for the disciple comes not in this world, but in the one to come. When the disciple has done everything he has been asked to do, he still does not put God into his debt.

> So you too, when you do all the things which are commanded you, say, 'We are unworthy slaves; we have done only that which we ought to have done' (Luke 17:10).

When the disciple realizes he is not everything today that he needs to be, he is granted the opportunity to begin anew each day with a greater determination to be better or more committed. One of the great blessings in serving God is the opportunity to start all over again with a clean record. The disciple says, "I am not what I ought to be; I am not what I'm going to be, but thank God, I am not what I was!" When one makes mistakes with civil law or has bad grades in academic work, the slate is seldom completely erased. The promises of God are comforting. They allow us to be today what we want to be in spite of past mistakes.

> 'Come now, and let us reason together,' says the Lord. 'Though your sins are as scarlet, they will be as *white as snow;* though they are red like crimson, *they will be like wool'* (Isaiah 1:18).

> *As far as the east is from the west, so far has He removed our transgressions from us.* Just as a father has compassion on his children, So the Lord has compassion on those who fear Him. For He Himself knows our frame; He is mindful that we are but dust (Psalm 103:12-14).

The ministries of Jesus and Paul are living testimonies that when one enlists to follow God, it is a lifetime commitment. The disciple is to be faithful until his task is complete. When the time comes for the disciple to depart his life, there should be before him some unfinished tasks and unfulfilled dreams for his life since the disciple must always see more frontiers to conquer for the Savior.

Discipleship which has to be defined and explained only in the past tense is in reality a pretense. The question for the disciple is not, "Did you follow?" or "Did you plan to follow?" It is rather, "Are you presently following the style of discipleship that is demanded by Jesus?"

Conclusion

The discipleship test is not an easy one to pass. If this test were given to Paul, Barnabas or the church at Thessalonica, they would pass. However, there are some individuals who could not pass the test. Demas was a fellow worker of Paul (Philemon 1:24), but he loved the world more than the cause of Christ. Demas did not fail because he did not live up to some church ordinance, but because he failed the discipleship test. At one time he could have passed the test, but that discipleship was in the past. Another failure can be demonstrated from John 12:42-43.

> Nevertheless many even of the rulers believe in Him, but because of the Pharisees, they were not confessing Him, lest they should be put out of the synagogue; for *they loved the approval of men rather than the approval of God.*

When one is more concerned about the applause of men than the approval of God, discipleship is impossible.

Reactions to the discipleship test can be varied. First, you can take the test dishonestly and not face up to the deficiencies of your life. Being honest about a relationship is one of the tough realities for the disciple. Second, you can react by trying to judge your grade by others in your class and reason that you aren't the best or the worst. To hope that God will grade on the "curve" is hope without expectation. It is comforting to know that God will judge all on an individual basis (2 Corinthians 5:10), but this cannot be used as an excuse to be like those around you. Third, you can hope that the course in Jesus' school of discipleship can be classified as an elective for a few "spiritual ones" and not a required course in the Christian curriculum. However, when one enrolls in Jesus' school of ministry with the anticipation of graduating, this is one of the core courses. It is not possible for you to get halfway through the course and decide to take a WP (withdraw while passing) and enroll at a later time. Fourth, you can take the test honestly, see your deficiencies, and use the experience as a motivation for improvement. When you grow from childhood to adulthood, you have to experience growing pains. It is God's desire to have His children full grown.

> And we proclaim Him, admonishing every man and teaching every man with all wisdom, that we may present *every man complete in Christ.* And for this purpose

also I labor, striving according to His power, which mightily works within me (Colossians 1:28-29).

When one realizes the seriousness of the commitment to follow Christ with all it entails, the teachings of Jesus become real.

Enter by the narrow gate; for the gate is wide, and the way is broad that leads to destruction, and *many* are those who enter by it. For the gate is small, and the way is narrow that leads to life, and *few* are those who find it (Matthew 7:13-14).

To make a real decision to follow is important if the war with Satan is to be won. There are several suggestions that will help you, the potential disciple, to be everything God desires you to be.

1. Make a commitment to the Lordship of Christ and be willing to accept His complete and unreserved control of your life. Christ is worthy of your allegiance. Desire to be everything He wants you to be and in every way He wants it, with no questions asked.

If you love Me, you will keep My commandments (John 14:15).

Not everyone who says to Me, 'Lord, Lord,' will enter the kingdom of heaven; but he who does the will of My Father who is in heaven (Matthew 7:21).

And why do you call Me, 'Lord, Lord,' and do not do what I say? (Luke 6:46).

I tell you no, but unless you repent, you will all likewise perish (Luke 13:3).

Everyone therefore who shall confess Me before men, I will also confess him before My Father who is in heaven. But whoever shall deny Me before men, I will also deny him before My Father who is in heaven (Matthew 10:32-33).

He who had believed and has been baptized shall be saved; but he who has disbelieved shall be condemned (Mark 16:16).

2. Make a commitment to be willing to be used by God in whatever way He decides to use you. The disciple must learn to "bloom where he has been planted" instead of always wanting to be somewhere else. When the disciple adopts this attitude, he is willing to be used in His service. The prayer will be answered.

96

Now when I came to Troas for the gospel of Christ and *when a door was opened for me in the Lord*, I had no rest for my spirit, not finding Titus my brother; but taking my leave of them, I went on to Macedonia. But thanks be to God, who always leads us in His triumph in Christ, and manifests through us the sweet aroma of the knowledge of Him in every place. For we are a fragrance of Christ to God among those who are being saved and among those who are perishing (2 Corinthians 2:12-15).

Paul saw three provisions by God given to him: (1) He was granted an opportunity ("door was opened"). (2) He was granted victory for his labor. (3) He became the aroma of Christ that gave the "knowledge of Him in every place."

3. Make a commitment to love people. The disciple is not called upon to love people where they are but to love them enough to see the potential they have by God's grace. You cannot love people without being willing to sacrifice for them. No one has ever really been effective for the Creator who has not loved His creation.

4. Make a commitment to be like Jesus in every way. The gospels need to be read on a regular basis with the attitude, "I will become what I read." The disciple should not be concerned so much with how much he has read as with how much he has applied what he has read. The gospels are the primary sources for developing Christlikeness and seeing practically the one he is to follow.

Great contributions and changes have been brought about by men who were dedicated to a cause they believed in. The price of progress and freedom has always demanded people of courage and conviction. Very few victories will be won by a half-hearted service to a goal. Communism is a good example of how an ideology can be spread in a relatively short period of time because men have committed themselves to a task. In a series of lectures delivered at the Institute of Marxism-Leninism in Yenan in July, 1939 (these were later published by the Foreign Languages Press in Peking in 1964 under the title, *How to Be A Good Communist*), Liu Shao-Chi outlined the important ingredients for being a good Communist. Those ingredients included: (1) Indoctrination. Every Communist should seek to be the best possible pupil of Marx and Lenin. (2) Dedication. Every Communist should submit one's life to the Party to the extent that he would die for it and not even allow his family to come between one and the Party. (3) Participation. Every Communist should be willing to be a part of every activity demanded by the Party.

97

The goals of the Party are clearly spelled out so every Communist will know what is expected of him. Liu Shao Chi said,

> What is our most fundamental duty as Party members? It is to achieve communism. As far as the Communist Parties of different countries are concerned, in each country it is for the Communist Party and the people there to transform it by their own efforts, and in that way the whole world will be transformed step by step into a communist world.[4]

The seriousness with which the Communists have approached their task has been unbelievable. One might have some serious differences with the Communist philosophy, but the effectiveness of spreading their message cannot be denied. A total commitment to what they believe to be the greatest truth for the world has produced a bondage to slavery for countless millions of people.

How can one who proclaims to be a follower of the greatest teacher the world has ever known and who believes he is participating in the oldest plan ever known approach this lifestyle half-heartedly? Surely the seriousness of serving a risen Savior, seeking the salvation of a lost world, and the realization of a judgment day should stir in all the followers a dedication and commitment that would shake the world in this generation. To have an opportunity to participate in such a grand vocation should bring about the kind of life that shows one's gratefulness. The disciple should be appreciative of the opportunity of his salvation and the opportunity to show its practical realities in his life.

> For by grace you have been saved through faith; and that not of yourselves it is the gift of God; not as a result of works, that no one should boast. For we are His workmanship, created in Christ Jesus for good works, which God prepared beforehand, that we should walk in them (Ephesians 2:8-10).

It is my prayer that this book on discipleship will affect you as much as it has me. The disciples of Jesus have a great task ahead of them: to reach the world. When the history books are written about our generation, will they say of our evangelistic efforts, "They could have but didn't." Someone has observed, "If the living knew what the dead know, we would evangelize the world in our generation."

---

[4]Liu Shao Chi, *How to Be A Good Communist.* (Foreign Languages Press of Peking, 1964), p. 35.

"The faith which was once for all delivered to the saints" (Jude 3) depends on men of faith to deliver it to other men. It takes believers to communicate the gospel.

> But having the same spirit of faith, according to what is written, *'I believed, therefore I spoke,'* we also believe, therefore also we speak (2 Corinthians 4:13).

I close with a very convicting quote by Bob Moorhead as it appeared in *Pulpit Helps.* May this be our attitude as we launch out to become what our Father wants us to be—a reflection of His image.

> *I'm a part of the following of the unashamed.* I have Holy Spirit power. The dye has been cast. I have stepped over the line. The decision has been made. I'm a disciple of His. I won't look back, let up, slow down, back away or be still.

> *My past is redeemed, my present makes sense, my future is secure.* I'm finished and done with low living, sight walking, small planning, smooth knees, colorless dreams, tamed visions, mundane talking, "chincy" giving, and dwarfed goals.

> *I no longer need pre-eminence*, prosperity, position, promotion, plaudits, or popularity. I don't have to be right, first, tops, recognized, praised, regarded or rewarded. I now live by presence, lean by faith, walk by patience, lift by prayer and labor by power.

> *My face is set*, my gait is fast, my goal is heaven, my road is narrow, my way is rough, my companions few, my Guide reliable, my mission clear. I cannot be bought, compromised, detoured, lured away, turned back deluded or delayed. I will not flinch in the face of sacrifice, hesitate in the presence of the adversary, negotiate at the table of the enemy, ponder at the pool of popularity, or meander in the maze of mediocrity.

> *I won't give up*, shut up, let up, until I have stayed up, stored up, prayed up, paid up, preached up for the cause of Christ. I am a disciple of Jesus. I must go till He comes, give till I drop, preach till all know, and work till He stops me. And when He comes for His own, He will have no problem recognizing me—my colors will be clear.[5]

---

[5]Bob Moorhead, *Pulpit Helps.* (Chattanooga, Tennessee), Vol. IX, No. 1, October, 1983.

Questions and Discussion Suggestions

For those who plan to use this book as classroom material, I suggest you discuss the content in the chapters prior to considering these questions and discussion suggestions.

Chapter 1: Rooted in God

1. What do we learn from other passages on God's eternal purpose? (1 Peter 1:20; Acts 2:23; Romans 8:28-29; 2 Timothy 1:9; Titus 1:2)
2. How did the pagan gods of the Old Testament affect human behavior?
3. How has God shown His desire to redeem and be with His people?
4. How is the word "knowledge" used in Hosea and in the gospel of John?
5. What is meant by the "image of God?"

Chapter 2: Manifested in Jesus

1. Study Colossians 1:15-2:3 and note the supremacy of Jesus.
2. How did Jesus reveal God in His life?
3. What did Jesus reveal about His Father in the sermon on the mount (Matthew 5-7)?
4. Study the gospel of Luke and see how Jesus is depicted as "going to Jerusalem." What did this have to do with His mission?
5. What did Jesus give up to become man? (Philippians 2:5-11; John 17:3; 2 Corinthians 8:9)

Chapter 3: Mark 1:17-20

1. What do fishers of men and fishers of fish have in common? Problems? Challenges? Expectations?
2. How is the word "disciple" used in the gospels as opposed to the rest of the New Testament?
3. Where did the early disciples believe that Jesus was leading them?
4. How can we be "transformed" into His image?
5. What are some of the actions of the disciples in Acts that would show their transformation?

Recommendation: Read *Aroma of Christ*, pages 39-46, by Jim

Woodroof to learn more on the idea of transformation.

Chapter 4: Mark 8:34-38

1. Summarize what the disciples learned, saw and did from Mark 1:20-8:34.
2. How was this material in Mark 1:20-8:34 important to their training as a disciple?
3. Find other events in the life of Peter when his speaking was used as an opportunity to teach him and other disciples.
4. Find other examples where Jesus said something and the disciples took it the wrong way (Matthew 16:6-12; John 4:10-11).
5. What are some of the decisions you have to make in following Jesus?

Chapter 5: Mark 10:28-30

1. How would you evaluate the man and his actions of Mark 10:17-22?
2. What are some of the hundred-fold blessings of the disciple?
3. What persecutions should today's disciple expect?
4. What does the disciple have to leave today in order to follow Jesus?
5. How does one balance the possession of wealth and at the same time follow Jesus? (Mark 10:25).

Chapter 6: Luke 9:57-62

1. What are some excuses given today for not following Jesus?
2. What personal responsibility does the disciple have to proclaim the kingdom?
3. What are some of the reasons why disciples quit plowing?
4. What are some suggestions for encouraging steadfastness and faithfulness?
5. What does working in the lives of others do for your life, attitude, example, and priorities?

Chapter 7: Luke 14:25-33

1. How can you maintain responsibilities to family and still follow Jesus?
2. How can the disciple maintain a daily consistency in following Jesus?
3. What will happen to the disciple when he forgets "the will of

God?" How can you keep it from happening?

4. How much should you know about what it means to follow Jesus before you begin?
5. In light of the stress on cross bearing (Mark 8:34; Luke 14:27), how is this translated into the disciple's life?

Chapter 8: Gospel of John

1. How does the gospel of John differ from Matthew, Mark and Luke in material, vocabulary, and purpose?
2. How can the disciple abide in the word on a consistent daily basis?
3. Discuss John 15. What are the implications of the vine and branches for the disciple? Note the meaning of John 15:2,6,8 and 16.
4. What are some of the challenges we face in loving one another?
5. Is there *really* a pattern of four elements of discipleship? Trace them back to God through Jesus. Are there other Old Testament men or women who fit the pattern? Luke 5:1-11 has the four elements of discipleship. List them.

Chapter 9: The Church in Acts

1. How did the teaching in the gospels form the foundation for the church in Acts?
2. What made the difference between the desertion in the hour of trial and the boldness of the same ones in Acts?
3. What is involved in preaching Jesus? Does the modern pulpit preach much about Jesus?
4. Has the church gained respectability at the price of dependability on God?
5. Why isn't a modern Acts being written today? What would we have to do to write it?

Chapter 10: Thessalonian Church

1. How do you harmonize the stress on the imitation with 1 Corinthians 1:10-17?
2. What are we to imitate from the lives of others?
3. What are some other passages which show the need for example? What does the need for example play in the qualification of leaders?
4. What are some idols that are worshipped by people professing to be disciples today?

5. What part does the teaching on the second coming of Christ play in daily discipleship? (See Mark 8:38)

Chapter 11: Paul

1. Discuss the background of Paul. (Philippians 3:4-11; Acts 22:1-10)
2. What were some of the problems and disappointments Paul experienced after he became a Christian? How did he not let these things cause him to defect?
3. What were some of the motivations that kept him going? (2 Corinthians 5:11,14)
4. What were some of his spiritual accomplishments in life?
5. Why did Paul become more prominent even though he had a later start than the other apostles?

Chapter 12: Barnabas

1. What influence did Barnabas have in the life of Paul? (Acts 9:27; 11:25; 13:2; 15:31-41)
2. Does Paul's description of love in 1 Corinthians 13:4-6 describe Barnabas?
3. What influence did Barnabas have in the life of John Mark? What would have happened to men like Paul and Mark had not Barnabas lived?
4. Why were the early Christians so generous with their possessions when they had only been Christians a short time? Does zeal and enthusiasm tend to wear off the longer a person is a Christian? How can you keep this from happening?
5. Can two spiritual men have a serious difference? (Acts 15:36-41) How did they solve their problems, and what is the application for today?

Chapter 13: Are You Following Jesus?

1. Is following Jesus an essential to discipleship? How do you know?
2. How do disciples show they are *really* followers of Jesus?
3. What are some of the compromises in leadership of the disciple that are being made today?
4. How can the disciple keep Jesus as leader in focus on a daily basis?
5. Can enough evidence be gathered from your neighborhood, school, place of work, and friends to convict you as being a

follower of Jesus? Would the evidence be circumstantial or concrete?

Chapter 14: Are You Working Spiritually in the Lives of Others?

1. Does the disciple have to work in the lives of others to be a follower of Jesus?
2. Is 2 Timothy 2:2 being fulfilled in your life?
3. What does spiritual reproduction have to do with your personal salvation?
4. What are the obstacles of working in the lives of others? What will happen to the church if we refuse to work with others in a personal way?
5. List the people whose lives you are presently working in to make them more like Jesus?

Chapter 15: Are There Things in Your Life That You Are Not Willing to Surrender in Order to Be A Real Disciple?

1. Do you believe one has to surrender all that he is to be a disciple?
2. What is the relationship of sin and the disciple today?
3. What are some of the daily battles that the disciple has with sin?
4. How can the disciple keep sin from finding a place again in his life?
5. Is it possible for one to become a part of the church and never really make a decision about sin? How would you decide whether or not this has taken place in your life?

Chapter 16: Is Your Discipleship Present Tense or Past Tense?

1. In light of this study of discipleship, how do you feel about your life for God?
2. What are the areas you plan to change and how and when do you plan to do it?
3. What part will the word of God play in your transformation? How do you plan to treat it differently than you have in the past?
4. Do you believe that God has a plan and purpose for your life? What is it?
5. How can you share this message of discipleship with others?

Notes

Notes

Notes

Notes

Notes

Notes

Notes

Notes

Notes

Notes

Notes